As Living Stones

My Five Years in Saudi Arabia

Marjory Henderson

Headline Books, Inc.
Terra Alta, WV

As Living Stones
My Five Years in Saudi Arabia

by Marjory Henderson

To order additional copies of this book or for book publishing
information, or to contact the author:

Headline Books, Inc.
P.O. Box 52
Terra Alta, WV 26764
www.HeadlineBooks.com

Tel: 304-789-3001
Email: mybook@headlinebooks.com

ISBN 13: 9781951556600

Library of Congress Control Number: 2021939184

To our Savior Jesus Christ who took me from religion to relationship, my mom who suggested I write the book, my husband Keith, and our sons Craig and Curtis who lived the book with me.

Content

Acknowledgments

The book would be incomplete without acknowledgments as there are others who have aided the process. First is my mother who encouraged me to write it using the weekly letters I sent to our family during our five years in Riyadh, Saudi Arabia. Second are my husband, Keith, and our sons Craig and Curtis who experienced all this with me. Patti Wood, a dear friend since Saudi Arabia days, aided by proofreading the manuscript. Roxanne Lee restored the old photographs. I have great joy in telling you about other friends in Riyadh who showed us what it looked like to walk with the Lord. All these people contributed to this memoir about my new life in Jesus Christ. It is no wonder that our Saudi Arabia group still has such a great love for each other as He used that time to "build us into His spiritual dwelling." As God tells us in 1 Peter 2:5: "You yourselves, as living stones, a spiritual house, are being built into a spiritual dwelling..." The writer acknowledges indebtedness to Wikipedia, *Aramco Handbook*, *Saudis: Inside the Desert Kingdom* by Sandra Mackey and *Colours of the Arab Fatherland* by Angelo Pesce.

Most of all I am indebted to the Lord Jesus who answered over and over when I asked "How should I say that?" or "How do these paragraphs link together?" I was pursued to write as He showed me how to write for His glory, to please my mom and to point others to Him. I also want to mention our friends, Carole and Fred Freeman and Harvey Dove, who were very prominent in my husband, our older son, and me, coming to know Jesus as Savior. Ken Smith, another Riyadh friend, wrote his memories. I used them to augment what I remember.

Dudley Woodberry, the first resident pastor in Riyadh, Saudi Arabia, and his wife Roberta also contributed memories. Cathy Teets, my publisher from Headline Books who patiently taught me what I did not know.

Introduction

Saudi Arabia. What do these words bring to mind? An ocean of sand? Oil? Mecca? Al Qaeda? If you are like many Westerners, that pretty much sums it up. But it was so much more than that! Halfway across the world, full of intrigue, holding both joyful and painful experiences, it became a second home for me. Continue reading and I will tell you my story, what it was like to move from the green of Colorado to the brown of Saudi Arabia, from having religion to having a relationship with the Lord.

Imagine with me fields of oil wells. Those oil wells began "the mad dash into the twentieth century," as Sandra Mackey phrased it in her book *Saudis: Inside the Desert Kingdom*. My husband was part of that mad dash, taking our two preschool-age sons and me along with him. He plunked us down in the midst of a nation where five-times-a-day calls to prayer were heard, where Islam was not just a religion but was a way of life. Unlike the democracy which had been part of my life since birth, the *Mattawa* (religious police) enforced *Sharia* law. Law based on the Koran. Law which ruled social, commercial, domestic, criminal, and political affairs, every aspect of each Muslim's daily life. Law which marked non-Muslims as infidels with the nation of Israel being especially scorned. Law which made it impossible to enter Saudi Arabia if one had "Israel" stamped on one's visa.

Many remember the attack on the World Trade Center on September 11, 2001, when they think of Saudi Arabia. The author personally heard a Muslim Background Believer in Christ say he had gone to flight school with some of the men who flew the planes on that day. He commented, "I wonder what would have happened if someone had told them about Jesus?"

On the Way

Fortunately, as a whole, we experienced positive interactions with Muslims after our move to Saudi Arabia. We found the Saudis very friendly and helpful even when they did not know us. Once, walking several blocks to the paved street with our baby and toddler to find a taxi, a man came from his villa to walk the block ahead of us. He had a taxi waiting when we got there. That was wonderful help as I, along with all the other women in the country, could not drive. Another time we were waiting for a taxi during a bad dirt storm. A taxi stopped, but I declined as there was already a male passenger in it. That could possibly involve a moral problem. He got out to give the taxi to us and walked himself.

The Saudis were also very curious and gracious as well as helpful. An illustration of their curiosity was the day two men, three women, and a young girl came to the gate, rang our doorbell, and then toured our yard! They left after looking over our toddler's tricycle and seeing him ride. Graciousness was shown when, on another day, as I visited the palace with some other expatriates, one of the three princesses made certain we understood it was not necessary to drink their strong cardamom-flavored coffee even though it was a part of their usual hospitality.

We had many positive interactions with the Saudis. So without further ado, let me tell you our story.

"Help, Lord! I have a two-year-old and a two-week-old son, and my husband just lost his job!" Even though I did not yet know Him as the One who died on the cross and came alive again to take the punishment for my sin, I was comforted by that prayer. I had the assurance He had heard and was answering. A month later, we were living in Riyadh, Saudi Arabia, and my husband had a new job.

As you can imagine, it was not easy for the grandparents. My Mom asked," Are you sure you want to do this?" My father-in-law later said, "I didn't think we'd ever see you again." But I felt comfortable with the move even though my husband and I were not typically adventuresome people.

My Mom used her creativity to maintain a connection with her grandsons through the years. She put records my sisters and I had as children onto tapes for them. She sent sticker books they thoroughly enjoyed, the ones that taught them the names of the various types of monkeys, dogs, and other animals. They even had a wooden puzzle of the United States and learned the names of the various states as they put it together. Oklahoma was always called "the gun!" She also made them green corduroy coats and purple embroidered western shirts.

My Mom and Dad with our sons

My parents were excited when a cassette tape from us would arrive. One was of our older son as he first began reading as a preschooler. On another, he was being interviewed by his Dad after a trip to Dirab, the city in which the Ministry of Agriculture Research Farm was located. "Did you talk a lot?"

"Yeah, I did! Yeah, I did!"

When I heard about the phone call asking my husband if he wanted to interview for the position, I was completely against the move. I could imagine myself trying to raise two young children with a scrub board to wash clothes and an icebox instead of a refrigerator. The Lord encouraged me. I asked my pastor how to determine the will of God. The next day, I found a woman with my husband's company, Ford Foundation, would provide a home with a stove, washing machine, refrigerator, freezer and furniture, even a gardener. Later we learned all three of them played bridge had and lived there for three years. She said we would be crazy not to go. Then we went to Denver to talk to the two men who interviewed my husband for the position. One of the men and his wife had lived in Riyadh for seven years. They were able to tell us more about living conditions congratulated themselves for finding someone who would take the position!

One convenience Ford Foundation did not supply was a driver. It would have made life easier since, as I mentioned before, no woman was licensed to drive in Saudi Arabia. One day, when I was out in our pickup with my husband, I began to complain mentally, I wish I had a driver. The Lord replied in a still, small voice inside me, "What are you complaining about? I'm taking care of you." He is so gentle with us. You can be certain that hearing from Him put a stop to my complaining!

Our older son also showed his displeasure with the move. He stayed with a neighbor while our possessions were being packed. Upon seeing his empty room when he returned, he exclaimed, "This makes me angry!" It struck me as humorous. He had probably heard me say that a few times!

After our long flight across the ocean, he amused me by excitedly commenting, "We're moving! We're moving!" It was not until he saw objects on the ground as the airplane whizzed by during landing that he recognized movement. He was a very well-behaved child to sit all that time with no idea why!

My Husband's Work

My husband's new position was working in agriculture for Ford Foundation. He would show farmers how to grow wheat with trickle irrigation. He had no idea what it would entail. In due time he learned there were three responsibilities: 1. Develop model growing practices on

My husband, two Saudis, sign saying "Ministry of Agriculture Wheat Program"

three farms 2. Use the developed practices on twenty private farms as demonstrations to other farmers 3. Train young Saudi men in the methods of farming and handling farm equipment. They would then act as extension agents between the Ministry of Agriculture and the farmers.

Most of the farm equipment was shipped disassembled. My husband and his co-workers felt very fortunate if all the pieces were there, even if they were not in the right places! They once

Donkey helping dig well

saw a driver bounce a box holding a land leveler off the back of a truck. No reason to use a ramp! The result was bent pieces but *"molish"* ("of no importance"). Nothing a hammer couldn't take care of!

It was no wonder the transition to machinery was difficult for the Saudis as their typical mode of farm work presented itself when we saw men digging a well with the help of a donkey. The method utilized a rubber basket that ran over a pulley. When signaled, the donkey would move forward to lower the bucket into the well. A man at the bottom would fill the bucket, after which the worker would again signal the donkey, which moved away from the well pulling the bucket to the surface to be emptied. You can imagine it took some time to dig a well approximately forty feet deep! During the process, it was the land owner's job to sit in the shade and watch!

Much of the wheat was pounded and made into round Pita bread. It was then baked on a paddle in an oven with an open flame. The bread became a favorite of mine! Grocery store pita bread in the States is no match for the from-the-oven-to-me bread I had there. Sometimes I was even able to buy it warm!

Sadly, my husband heard of many people being poisoned after eating bread from wheat treated with insecticide. The hospital was full. Hospital personnel had to put beds outside. For that reason, Ford Foundation never treated the wheat.

Ford also maintained their ethical policies by refusing to give bribes. That practice was used by many other companies in order to keep government officials happy while at the same time staying within the dictates of U.S. law.

Interesting things happened on my husband's trips to visit the farmers. He would travel with a Saudi counterpart who acted as translator. One farmer asked, "Is Jesus in the Bible?" When he was told, "Yes," he replied, "I just cry when I read about Him in the Koran."

Since he was on a friendship basis with the farmers, one invited him and some of his other friends to eat cantaloupe and honeydew melon. They all sat on the ground on both sides of a sheet of plastic that held the food. My husband ate a great quantity and then stopped. The farmer said, "Don't be ashamed. Eat more! Eat more!" He ate more. Then he noticed some of the other men were pushing themselves back from the plastic sheet as they finished. As he started scooting back, the farmer grabbed him by the leg and pulled him up again!

The farmers honored my husband in two different ways. One was tossing the tongue of the camel they were having for lunch on his plate! "What did you do?!" I asked.

"I tossed it onto someone else's plate!"

Another honor was hearing, "You are of my tribe." That was an extremely great honor for a foreigner to receive as their tribes were very important to them.

He was also honored when a farmer sent a telegram to the king. It began, "Your royal highness, may you live forever" and concluded, "Thank you for bringing the American." Ford Foundation agreed it should not be copied.

My husband does have a paper with written permission to be the first non-Saudi licensed to drive a truck. It is signed by the Minister of Interior, who later became king.

After eating, the farmers thanked God for the food ("*bismillah*") rather than thanking Him before eating, as is the custom in the West.

All eating was done with the right hand. The left was used for bathroom purposes. This posed a severe problem for some as the punishment for theft was having the right hand amputated.

The living conditions were not good on those trips. My husband humorously once said, "It might not be possible to find a place where the owner had previously managed a hotel, but it would be nice to stay at a place where the owner had at least STAYED in a hotel." During some of the trips, my husband and his co-workers slept on the flat roof where it was a little cooler. They had to walk to a gas station to use the restroom. On one occasion, when they returned to the hotel, they found the cook holding a chicken with his feet as he cut it up. The men's feet are filthy as they wear sandals and walk on very dusty land! The group decided to live off canned goods!

On the same trip, they saw women with an ox. The ox dragged a big, flat, round stone about the size of a car wheel around and around a flat area that acted as the threshing floor. Gideon from Bible times did the same. "Gideon, the son of Joash, was threshing wheat at the bottom of a winepress to hide the grain from the Midianites" (Judges 6:11). Despite Gideon living thousands of years earlier, there was only one difference. It was women working with the ox then throwing the wheat into the air so the chaff would be blown away. They ran off when they saw several carloads of men approaching. As in Bible times (Ruth 2:2), farmers left wheat along the edge of the fields to be gleaned by the poor.

Regarding another trip, he said, "I foolishly took some advice on the availability of food at the hotel and about starved." He could not hack the barley soup with chunks of camel meat and pieces of sheep stomach served in a restaurant with a dirt floor, tin walls, and wooden benches. The hotel manager was very happy to inform him they had water!

In contrast, he was also an advisor on landscaping the grounds of the King Faisal Hospital. That hospital, one of the best in the world, was top-notch in every way, including a lapis lazuli mosaic portrait of King Faisal with diamond flecks in his eyes.

Our Arrival

Author and my sons outside typical Saudi villa

All of that was to come. The immediate need was to ac-
climate to our new home. We had shipped what we felt were
essentials by air and sent the rest by boat. When the later ship-
ment arrived almost six months later, we were surprised our
older son was so excited to see his potty chair. He and it were
almost inseparable for several days as he dragged it from room
to room with him! I guess he was tired of my suspending him
above the toilet when he had to use it.

Unlike two of our dear friends, our belongings arrived in-
tact. Describing the scene in which they unwrapped all their
broken Indian pottery: "We just kept saying, 'Earthly treasure.
Earthly treasure.'"

We had actually deplaned in Beirut, Lebanon, where we
spent a week getting acclimated to leaving our culture. My husband also received orientation for his upcoming job responsibilities. One of the men who had interviewed my husband for
the job flew to Saudi Arabia with us to help us get settled in our
new home. We became good friends and visited him and his

wife in Beirut each time we spent time there. His wife always cooked a pork roast for us. It was a great treat as we could not buy pork in Saudi Arabia. I still have the recipe she would cook. Delicious! But not for the Saudis! A young Muslim woman told me a little about her trip to the States. When she realized she had eaten pork, she vomited!

We landed in Saudi Arabia and began to settle, decorating our walls with posters I got from a travel agency. I found that although Riyadh was not a difficult place to live, getting there had been really hard. Through a mix-up, we did not receive notification of the two nights layover in Europe stipulated in the contract. Instead, we spent twenty-three hours in airports or on airplanes. It seemed like every time one child did not need to eat; the other needed to go to the bathroom! I have never been so tired!

Having a series of house boys added to the ease of our lives. Most everyone hired someone at least part-time as all vegetables and fruit needed to be washed in Clorox water due to the danger of cholera as well as other household tasks I did not need to do when keeping my home in the States.

The dirt streets meant dusting several times a day for cleanliness was necessary. An American during a return visit to Riyadh said his wife still occasionally exclaimed, "There's no dust!" They had been back in the States for a year and she was still not used to that! Likewise, after our return, it took me years to get over the habit of pushing the tops of canned goods with my index finger to see if they were bulging, an indication the food was spoiled.

Grocery Shopping

As we acclimated, we were very pleased with the supermarket although it was vastly different than what we experienced in the States. The storekeeper trusted his customers completely. Everyone bought food on account just by signing their names, even if the shopkeeper had never before seen them. One day my husband joked with him, saying, "I won't be able to pay my bill unless I get paid."

"*Molish! Molish!*" ("No problem! No problem!") he replied. After I admired a candle, the manager came out to our pickup saying, "Mrs. Henderson, I would like you to accept this with our compliments."

Powdered Nido, the only milk available, tasted terrible! We had to add chocolate or strawberry syrup to make it drinkable. When we prepared for our move back to the States, I told our sons, "The milk tastes so good you don't need to put flavoring into it." I was all for cutting down the sugar they ingested.

We kept our sons entertained as we shopped by letting them ride "like a fireman," one standing on one side of the cart and the other on the other side. They were rewarded by little treats like Pez for good behavior. It is amazing how some products cross time and culture!

We were able to get almost any item we wanted, although not necessarily when we wanted it. For instance, we found fruit for fruit cake months after Christmas.

We learned to be very flexible when it came to ingredients. Sometimes we said, "Anything can substitute for anything." Celery, which often needed a substitute, was highly prized when it was available. After finding some at the vegetable *Souk* (the conservative shopping area in town), a friend asked me, "Could I just have the leaves?" They would become a prized ingredient in her Thanksgiving dressing. To this day, I often think of that experience when I buy celery. And I sometimes smile at my husband when we are cooking together and say, "Anything substitutes for anything" when we do not have an ingredient listed in a recipe.

I went to the vegetable *Souk* fairly often as it was the source of the best qualities of fruits and vegetables. There were always men from Yemen there with baskets to hold the vegetables for a shopper. My husband got a big smile one day when he acted like he was going to put our younger son in a basket to be carried. Humor has a way of breaking down cultural walls.

I would often buy apples as for a long period, apples and milk made up our sons' diets. Our doctor in the States said not to be concerned about it, to just make certain they took a multivitamin. The diet provided a bit of humor. I told our older son, who was making a habit of only partially eating his apple, "You can't have another apple until you finish every bit of that one." His response: "But the core would taste so awful!"

We saw shopping from a Saudi viewpoint when a man mentioned he did not like England because you had to "queue up" all the time. There were lines for everything! I really had to laugh inside. A couple of weeks earlier, while vegetable shopping in the *Souk*, I was at the cash register and not able to pay due to the fact several people standing behind me were sticking their arms over my shoulders, holding money out for their purchases.

Entertainment

My husband and sons in the sand dunes

Some entertainment in Riyadh was similar to what we had experienced in the States. I spent time with friends and played bridge as I had in my past life. Other entertainment was completely different. For instance, I went to horse races which sometimes included a camel race and was very thankful when a Chinese food restaurant opened. I no longer had to walk by the area of open sewage which was outside the previous restaurant we all frequented! In contrast, appealing odors greeted me each time I visited Chicken Street, where rotisserie chickens and *swarma* (leg of mutton) were roasted over open fires along the sidewalks.

We had desert picnics about 110 kilometers away from our city. Adults, as well as children, enjoyed sliding down an area of sand dunes about 40-50 kilometers wide made of reddish-brown sand. Our older son took delight in being buried in the sand up to his neck during some of our times there with friends.

We were quite creative as various needs presented themselves. How were we to go to the bathroom in an area where Porta-Potties were unknown and there were no trees to hide us? Necessity is the mother of invention! A group of women formed a circle holding up their long dresses to block the friend in the center who did what was necessary. Each of us had her need met before we rejoined our husbands. Mission accomplished!

We collected souvenirs on some of those trips: Desert roses, some as big as chairs, which looked like their namesake and were formed from sand, two pieces of petrified wood measuring about five inches by twelve inches, small petrified clamshells so numerous I could just scoop them off the ground. My husband found half a clamshell about fist-sized with the other half about a foot away. Since Saudi Arabia has only scattered rain at the most and some years nearly none, it was so dry I would call our sons outside to see even one cloud. That being the situation, all those shells indicated to me there had been a worldwide flood.

Desert Rose

One time on the way back to town, a man needing to get to his family flagged us down as his car no longer would run. It was safe to give him a ride. We certainly would not have considered that in the States!

An international cooking group in which the women took turns making culinary dishes from their home countries proved to be something I enjoyed. I told someone, "When it's my turn, I'm going to demonstrate cooking while holding a baby with a toddler tugging on your leg!" We eventually wrote a cookbook. I still have some of the recipes. One is a delicious meatloaf from a Filipino friend. It is a favorite of mine when we have company as it can be cooked in the crockpot to serve after church.

We also enjoyed seeing Yemenis, natives of the southern end of the Arabian Peninsula, build a villa behind outs. Left without oil, the Yemenis migrated north early in the oil boom to become the backbone of Saudi Arabia's manual labor force. They were small men dressed in skirts and turbans. While working, they would pull the backs of their skirts between their legs and tuck them in front, an illustration of "gird up your loins" (Exodus 12:11) when the Israelites left Egypt. "Now you shall eat it in this manner: with your loins girded, your sandals on your feet, and your staff in your hand, and you shall eat it in haste. It is the LORD'S Passover." Whether Yemeni or Israeli, girding up the loins expedited movement. In some ways, Saudi Arabia made the Bible come to life.

The owner of the home gave my sons and me permission to tour their villa. Generally, Muslims did not like to have their pictures taken. They considered them to be graven images. I asked if I could take a picture and one of the workers agreed. Another motioned me outside so I could take a picture of him slapping cement on the house. It was the last picture on the roll, so I told another man wanting his picture taken, "*Halas. Anna asppha. Bucra enshala*." ("Finished. I'm sorry. Tomorrow if God wills"). "If God wills" was the phrase almost always added to a future event as no one could know for certain it would happen. The prints I had made for them were probably their first pictures of themselves.

Enjoyable as it was to watch the construction, we really did not enjoy being awakened as soon as it was daylight by jackhammers as the men flattened the hill on which to build the villa. But, yes, you can learn to sleep through it. I could also learn to sleep through a call to prayer coming from a loud-speaker in a mosque near our home before sunrise each day!

Thobs and Abyaas

My husband worked with Saudis daily. My first opportunity to talk with anyone from our host nation was at a dinner given by the Deputy Minister of Agriculture. When I walked in and saw the men in their *thobs* (robes) and *gutras* (head coverings), I thought, "Good heavens! I can never communicate with these people!" The women were not veiled. They did put on their *hijabs* (face and head coverings with tiny slits which allowed them to see) and *abyaas* (garments made of black cloth which covered them from the top of their shoulders to below their ankles) when they left. Somehow I felt like the people under those veils were different. They WERE different than most Saudis because they were Western-oriented and educated. They did hold to the tradition that men and women were in different rooms. The women I talked with disliked the *hijabs* immensely.

Some of the Saudis we knew were very conservative regarding veiling. Others not. Even those with American wives did not all feel the same about the issue. Many of the wives veiled only their hair, and did that only to keep their husbands from being criticized. Their husbands would have been very willing to have their wives not wear veils. The opposite extreme was the husband who told his American wife to burn the pictures of an American friend who had

Woman in hijab and abyaa

23

just married a Saudi because she was not veiled in the pictures. Imagine the hurt that would have caused both the wife and her friend!

The dress code for the women was designed so a woman would not sexually arouse a man whom she passed on the street, but a *hijab* and an *abyaa* were unable to keep the men's minds from impure thoughts. I remember vividly waiting in the car with my sons while my husband went into a shop. The three men standing near our car moved their heads slowly from one side to the other as they watched several completely veiled women pass by. The women were not dressed from the top of their heads to their ankles in their minds.

The Lord protected me one evening when I put myself in grave danger by riding in a taxi without either of our sons. Even though I dressed very conservatively (high neckline, long sleeves, and long skirt), I was considered to be a loose woman by some of the Saudis because I did not wear the *hijab* and *abyaa*. Taking a child when going out was protection for me. That evening I intended to go just a short way to pick up a young woman to go to a party. Since there was no way to contact her, I didn't know she was not at home. I decided to go on to the party by myself as my husband was already there. I could not contact him and he would worry. I got lost and gave the driver directions that caused him to drive around until we came to a ditch we could not cross. I saw the villa across the ditch and said, "*Henna*" ("here"), indicating he should stop. He assumed the worst and started to reach for me. The Lord was my protector as I said, "*La!*" ("No!") He backed away. I got out of the taxi, crossed the ditch, and was soon safe inside. I am so thankful the Bible says of our God, "He searches my path…"! (Psalm 139:3). He "laid [His] hand upon me"! (Psalm139:5). That is the only time I have ever hidden something from my husband.

Marriage Customs

Sadly, Islam promotes male superiority. Mohammed, in *Sura* (chapter and verse) 4:34 of the Koran, states: "Men have authority over women because Allah has made one superior to the other and because they spend their wealth to maintain them. They guard their unseen parts because Allah has guarded them. As for those from whom you fear disobedience, admonish them and send them to beds apart and beat them." And further "*Sura* 4:2 states, "If you fear you cannot treat orphans [orphan girls] with fairness, then you marry other women who seem good to you: two, three, or four of them. But if you fear you cannot maintain equality among them, marry only one or any slave girls you may own. This will make it easier for you to avoid injustice." Needless to say, multiple wives were often intensely competitive for the attention of their husband. Barren women suffered greatly as a woman's supreme task was to produce and care for children. If this was not achieved, it often meant a divorce which was easily obtained. All that was needed was to pronounce three times, "I divorce you. I divorce you. I divorce you."

Sandra Mackey tells of "countless Saudi women shake their beads and click their tongues at me as they told me how much they pity Western women because we lack the security Saudi women have within their families.

And they can look forward to old age. According to Mackey, "Old age may well be the most satisfying period of a woman's life. After a lifetime of serving men, she is accorded great honor in her family. Sons revere their mothers. Younger women in the household fall under the authority of the matriarch. He husband can become solicitous of her needs."

She no longer needs to fear divorce. A woman I met at a party and her husband had a more Western view of marriage. She had moved to the States with him the day after they married so he could attend college. The thought of another wife was no part of their marriage. She had gotten used to not wearing a veil and did not like them. I was amazed at her command of English, which she had learned watching television hour after hour because there had been nothing else for her to do.

Jaffa, Haile, Obeid, and Mohammed

While her fluency in English amazed me, my minimal Arabic would not have amazed anyone! It was a blessing each of our house boys and our gardener spoke a little English. My Arabic was limited to just a few words. "*La*" ("no"), "*awa*" ("yes"), "*kater flus*" ("too much money") which was useful in bargaining in the *Souk*, and "*swaya swaya*" ("slower slower"), which helped in conversing with taxi drivers. *Yameen and shamall* indicated whether to go right or left. I did know enough of the language to shout "*Moffi mook!*" ("No brain!") as a truck driver drove by, passing too close to our sons as they played in a vacant lot! After that experience, I humorously congratulated myself on my command of the language! But I applied *Moffie mook* to myself in telling an Arab girl when she asked me why I did not speak more Arabic.

We found it worked best to have a house boy who could understand my directions without understanding family conversations. Jaffa, our first house boy, possessed both qualities. He was also very good with our young sons. He even let them ride on the vacuum sweeper as he cleaned! As he served us at a dinner party one evening, I called him, "Mr. Jaffa." An American woman who had lived overseas many years objected to me giving him that title. In my mind, it was right to call him what he had suggested when I asked. His is a very sad story. He died as a result of drinking cologne for the alcohol content. One could only guess what happened to his two wives.

Haile our house boy

Haile was the epitome of hard work. He came by his own choice at 6:45 a.m. I would have preferred to be asleep at that time after often getting up during the night with our sons! He vacuumed, dusted, and scrubbed floors, appliances, and shelves, as well as washing down the outside of our villa. Except for a fifteen-minute break, he did not stop until lunch and then worked until about 2:00 p.m. when he was supposed to quit. I encouraged him to rest more. Instead, he asked if I had any ironing he could do and requested I buy some stove and window cleaner!

Obeid, our favorite houseboy, lived in the small servants' quarters behind our villa. He had an unusual ability—he was able to chop five pounds of onions without his eyes tearing. I did not have that ability! One time our older son came into the kitchen and thought I was weeping. I explained it was just because I was cutting onions. His soft-hearted comment was, "The next time you cut onions, I'll come out and cry with you!"

Even though Obeid was only seventeen years old when he began to work for us, he had a sense of purpose and attended classes from 6:00 to 10:00 each evening. His devotion to learning was not unusual. I sometimes saw young men standing under lampposts to study as there was no electricity in their homes. Obeid planned to go to school until he was nineteen years old. His parents sent him from Yemen to Saudi Arabia when he was thirteen since it was an opportunity for him to have a better life. It amazed me to think of his parents thrusting Obeid out at that tender age! His leaving us to take a job in a bookstore made me very glad.

Mohammed, the gardener the company hired for us, spoke a little English as well. Our toddler son had a close relationship with him. He would run to meet him, calling, "Hammed! Hammed!" Mohammed would bounce him on his knee or wriggle his tongue so our son could try to catch it. Mohammed watered the grass by squatting and holding the hose. You can tell grass was a scarce commodity in Saudi Arabia! He would then fill a can with water for our son to run back and forth, watering the flowers. He would then mimic our son, saying, "Rock…Squeeze." The second step of the routine was our son laying his cheek on the rock and saying, "Mmmm," which Mohammed mimicked as well.

All of our family had a relationship with Mohammed. One cold day I loaned him my coat. When he returned it, he brought me a bronze bracelet that depicted the Don Quixote legend which he had purchased in the *Souk*. I still value that bracelet. It has been over 45 years since we left Saudi Arabia, and I still sometimes pray for Haile, Obeid, and Mohammed.

Languages

I think it would be quite an interesting study to learn about a family by just knowing a small child's first hundred words. For instance, one of our younger son's first words was "*henna*" ("here") which he had heard me say many times when we arrived at our destination by taxi. He endeared himself to the daughter of an Arab friend when he used the word to indicate he wanted to go to the end of the swimming pool as she gave him swimming lessons. It also was possible to tell he was not an only child by his use of "mine" and "yours." He tried to sing the alphabet song "A, B, D, E," which he had heard his brother singing. On one occasion, his brother insisted he be given the Bible he received from friends saying, "I'm going to explain it all to him!" So he learned the word "Bible." When his brother told him, "Say thank you," it came out as "Ank koo."

Awareness of two languages influenced our older son's thinking. Being a gregarious little toddler who sometimes dropped the "s" in a word, he would walk up to people and ask, "Do you peak English?" Regardless of the answer he would then walk away, his curiosity satisfied. One of our conversations about Heaven amused me. He was accustomed to being around people who spoke only a little English. When he asked about Heaven, "How, when we see each other, will we get over to each other?" In other words, "How will we transport ourselves?" I told him I was sure God would tell us. He replied, "Maybe Jesus speaks a little bit of English."

Our younger son was sometimes very creative in his use of language. When we arrived at a friend's villa, he exclaimed, "Spiders tickle me!" He was expressing the fact his feet had fallen asleep as they hung over the edge of the car seat. Another time he and his brother were tired and lay down on the back seat of our car. His brother was accusing him of taking more than his share of the space. His reply, "It's just my dumb body!" It illustrated to me he knew he was more than a body. Amazing for a preschooler!

Our sons became very used to hearing people speaking Arabia all around them. Once when our family was in an airport for a vacation in the States, the older one kept jerking his head to the side. It looked like something was seriously wrong with him. When I asked about it, though, his reply was, "I don't like it when everybody speaks English; you think everyone is talking to you!"

That was definitely true in Riyadh. English was directed at us on the streets and both parties tried their best to bridge the language barrier. Pronunciations sometimes differed even when the word was known to both the speakers. Arabs cannot pronounce the letter "P," so the menu in a restaurant read, "Mama Burgers" and "Baba Burgers." Likewise, a taxi driver could not understand my directions to a villa by the Pepsi plant. He asked a man on the street who told him "Bebsi." There was no problem understanding that!

In addition to pronunciation difficulties translating from Arabic to English was problematic. Sandra Mackey wrote: "Moslem is also spelled Muslim. Mohammed can be spelled Muhammed, Muhamed, or Muhadi. I have seen sixteen different spellings for the city of Jeddah.

Contact with Royalty

In the States, I would have never have had an opportunity to work with a member of President Nixon's family, yet in Saudi Arabia, I was hired to speak English with a princess! She was preparing for her time in the States. We had a discussion about the number of times I would go each week. Although we eventually reached a compromise, it was easy to see she was not used to being told "no." It is hard for a person with no responsibilities to understand another's need to care for home and children.

At our first session, she wanted to talk about bath mats! She was very impressed with the variety she saw when she was in California for three months. She asked me to bring her some when we returned from vacation, which I did.

As the Saudis are very hospitable, she invited me to stay for lunch. After eating from the huge quantity of food that was served, we washed our hands. The maid dried them with a towel custom to pray afterward. Then poured perfume onto them. That was to remove any smell of food. I called my husband to tell him our son and I would be late returning home. He replied, "You don't have to talk that way with me." Without realizing it, I had talked the way you do to people who do not understand English. Very slowly and enunciating each syllable! I had earlier been amused at his talking over the phone like that to people with whom he worked when there was no need to do so.

I am certain another reason the princess wanted to meet with me was to alleviate boredom. Women did not get out of their homes often. I saw probably 100 men to one woman in the *Souk*, the conservative shopping area in town. There were not many in the other shopping areas either.

And boredom was probably the reason I began receiving up to twelve phone calls each day. The call would begin, "What is your name?" to which I would reply, "Puddentain." They were unable to see the humor! Asking the gardener to talk to the caller to make certain she did not really want something caused them to call less frequently.

Not many people had phones, and if you did, there was another problem. The code in the telephone book needed to be cracked. For instance, the Ford Foundation, my husband's employer, was listed in the twelve pages of "Establishments." Pepsi sodas were under "F" for "Factory." Canada Dry sodas were under "C" for "Company." The phone book also listed "Confidential Information." Could one call for a good gossip session or find out the nitty-gritty on a sheik? Hundreds of them could be found under the "S" section! Directions were given for using the phone, "Insert the index finger in the finger hole and rotate in a clockwise direction. Hold for four seconds. Withdraw the finger." Of course, there were no listings for women.

I had another very interesting look at the royal culture when visiting a neighbor. Her guest was the adopted daughter of the king. In that position, she was treated very well, but not like one of the king's natural-born children. Every one of those children had an adopted child as a companion. Each would learn royal behavior by ruling over the companion. This girl, at thirteen years old, was about to be married. She would be expected to bear a child in a year or less. That seemed very dangerous to me. She seemed to be quite happy with the situation. Her future husband was the financial advisor for a prince. He was 26 years old. He had given her 2,000 *riyals* (Saudi dollar bills) as a wedding present with which she had purchased a gold necklace, a watch, and two gold rings. She allowed him to put one of the rings on her finger, so that meant he had touched her hand. She told my friend she answered his questions by saying "Yes" or "No." She was too shy to speak anything more. He also gave her father 5,000 *riyals* for her. She did not know where they would live after marriage. They might live in the servant quarters, or her husband might live in the servants quarters and she in the upstairs of the palace.

It seems strange to us to marry someone chosen by one's parents. The advantage is the parents know the family background. They do not decide only on an emotional basis. A Saudi acquaintance of ours had been divorced. Her parents decided they did not approve of him after all. He was going to have to save up more than a year's salary again as dowry before he could marry another woman.

The choice of marriage being arranged by the family is part of not thinking of oneself as an individual but in the context of family. But that is not all that seemed strange to me. First cousin marriages were sought as group solidarity was ensured. In addition, men were considered to be descendants of their fathers and paternal grandfathers only. That again seemed like a slight to the women of the society. The oldest male member decided what was in the best interests of the family. He dictated the role each individual was to play, even whom one married, where one lived, whether one pursued an education and one's occupation. Definitely not a democracy!

In the States, I would have absolutely no opportunity to be invited to the White House, yet I, along with other expatriate women, was invited to the palace for a Saudi royal wedding! We were greeted by the queen then taken to the roof. There were probably 100 women gathered. Excitement built. Then the wedding began!

First in the bridal procession were ten Ethiopian women in blue dresses and white veils. They were beating drums. Then came what corresponded to the flower girl and ring bearer in an American wedding. Then came the bride with a woven veil approximately ten feet long. Many relatives followed her. The dresses were fantastic! The materials were solid in color. Some were decorated with beads and sequins. Others were bejeweled in very intricate patterns. The dresses the bride and the King's second wife wore were styled very much as one would see in an American wedding. But there was a great difference. The bride's dress was decorated with diamonds and her mother's with emeralds! We sat from about 7:00 p.m. to about 10:00 p.m., then ate the superabundant, very decoratively arranged meal. Afterward, there was a musical group and some dancers.

It was special to be greeted by the queen as we arrived, but the really big moment was seeing the king. I had such great respect for him due to what he had done for all his people. I was almost breathless as he came down the aisle where we were standing on chairs to see. There were probably 1,000 people in attendance.

There were shifts of eating. The expatriates dined first, then another group ate off our plates, another group ate after them, and so on until the Bedouins were called in to finish what remained!

The bride sat on a platform while women around her played bongo drums. The event organizer got two women at a time on the platform to dance for the happiness and fertility of the bride. A Western woman gained my respect as she was one of the first to dance. She later became a very good friend. As we left, the organizer made all of us expatriates dance. I was really glad to see I did better than I thought I would!

I left something behind. During the evening I became very hot because people were pressed so closely together. I slipped off the pajama bottoms, which I had worn under my long dress, thinking we would be outside where it was cold. I cannot imagine what the servant who found them thought! Probably he held them up with disdain and said something like, "These must belong to one of those crazy expatriate women!"

Neighbors

Seeing the culture through visits to neighbors' homes was interesting as well. Our gracious Saudi neighbors invited us over for dinner with eighteen other people. We knew that meant we would eat about 12:00 p.m. The invitation was for 9:00 p.m. so, appropriately, we did not go until 9:30. We sat around talking, eating nuts, and playing bridge until dinner. There was an enormous quantity of food included a whole sheep with the head surrounded by rice, chicken, shrimp, and six or seven other items plus two desserts and fruit. We stayed until almost 3:00 a.m. as they did not serve the tea and coffee, the signal for dismissal, until that time. I was awake again at 6:00 a.m. to care for our sons. I told my husband I had taken longer naps than that!

Neighbors with a huge house and six small rooms in a motel-like arrangement behind their villa invited my sons and me to visit. We sat out in one of the small rooms with a young man we had earlier seen with a hunting falcon, two elementary-age girls, and the father. The room had rugs covering the floor and cushions for seating. The father showed me through their expensively decorated home. One of the rugs was Chinese. A friend told me she had seen a similar rug priced way over $200.00 per square meter. Their rug was probably 6 square meters. He said they preferred to live in the small rooms then go into the house to sleep. That probably was more comfortable for them due to their having lived in tents as Bedouins.

When another family invited our sons and me to their home, we just stood and smiled at each other. At least, I think they were smiling. We could not see their faces through the *hijabs*. Their giggles were a clue, though. They kept motioning me to crouch down on their rug. I crunched down with my bottom resting on my heels. After a short time, they graciously had me sit. I had forgotten all the Arabs I had ever seen squatted. They must have developed muscles I had not. I certainly could not have maintained that position for long!

My sons with the porridge-making neighbor

Do you remember the story *Goldilocks and the Three Bears*? After reading the story to our sons a number of times, we wondered what porridge was. A single Canadian man in the next villa offered to make us some for breakfast. We enjoyed our time with him but were rather disappointed to find porridge is just good ole American oatmeal.

Our older son assisted me by remembering names. Since he was young, all names were new to him, it was no harder for him to remember "Raja" than to remember "Jane." He did mistakenly tell us his classmate's name was "Enchilada." It turned out to be "Ann Charlotta!"

My Husband's Counterpart

Another look at the culture came when we spent an evening with the counterpart who translated for my husband when they worked with the farmers. As custom dictated, my husband was in the room for men. I was across the hall in the room for women. It was not unusual for a villa to have two doors, one for men and the other for women, although that particular one did not. I found one of his sisters particularly interesting as she was studying physics at the women's university. She intended to attend medical school. Her field of study would have to be gynecology or pediatrics since a woman would not be allowed to examine a man or vice versa. As strange and unworkable as it seems to us, if a woman needed a specialist and only a male was available, the doctor could not examine the woman. He could only listen as her husband described her symptoms.

Having the counterpart made work much easier for my husband. He not only translated but helped my husband understand the intricacies of the culture. On one occasion, hundreds of bags of fertilizer arrived from Germany with one being damaged. Saudis are proud and desire to save face. My husband's question to his counterpart, "Would it be acceptable for me to talk to the Deputy Minister of Agriculture about the situation, or would it make the warehouse manager lose face?" The counterpart assured him there would be no problem if he talked with the Deputy.

Saving face was also involved when we heard 200,000 pieces of mail had gone up in flames. The disaster was never publicly acknowledged. Nor were scorching weather, floods, or wind storms ever mentioned in the newspaper. Only the best face was to be presented in all circumstances.

Since saving face was not a problem when one was in the States. Saudis had a swinging time while there. On his return to Saudi Arabia, my husband's counterpart was having problems adjusting to the culture after being gone for seven years. He, along with other returning students, missed the large stipend the government gave. He received approximately $4,000 a year on return to the country. He was also committed to work for the government for a period of time.

He was unmarried. Many students did marry in the States since the dowry for a bride was about $5,000 in Saudi Arabia. This presented a problem which the government eventually attacked by taking away the benefits of Saudi citizenship if one married a foreigner. The problem was partially solved as Saudi women became more attractive to the educated Saudi men when it became possible for them to get an education in Saudi Arabia.

The counterpart was a tribe leader's son and, as such, was responsible for entertaining if his father was away. At age nine or ten, he talked with and entertained leaders from other tribes. What a responsibility for a pre-teen!

His tribe was constantly on the move, generally traveling into Syria. When they settled for one year, he was able to go to boarding school, a very different education than he had up to that point. Generally, a teacher had traveled with them to teach the children in the group. He had a love for learning and was the first of their tribe to graduate from high school. He then worked with an airline which enabled him to fly to the States where he settled. His wife told me because of the difference in culture, she did not think he had spoken to a girl for the first year he was there.

Adjustment to Saudi Culture

In contrast to the counterpart, my husband and I adjusted to Saudi Arabia with relatively little difficulty. I realized I was basically doing what I would have been doing in the States. I was raising two small children. We did buy a box of very expensive chocolates telling ourselves we could eat one only when we were discouraged.

One time I did get really upset. I was in tears in our prayer group due to the way some of the Saudi men yelled at me when they drove by, even though I dressed modestly. Soon after, I read, "The Lord will fight for you and you have only to be silent" (Exodus 14:14) to our sons in their children's Bible storybook. The Lord broke the discouragement! The experience showed me the power of God's Word even when it was in a storybook rather than a Bible. Again I had peace in being in Riyadh.

Many did not have that same peace. Why did they stay? *Flus.* (Money.) In order to get employees in that difficult working situation, companies paid a great deal of money. Although that was only one of the reasons we stayed, the money eventually paid for our sons' college educations.

Some of the expatriates also had difficulty adjusting. I remember one woman married to a Saud who could not seem to stop crying. I gave her one of the two canned hams a friend had given me. The friend could get ham by mail through her and her husband's Army Post Office, which did not go through customs. It's amazing how much it helps to beat the system occasionally!

Saudi Arabia was both exciting and exhausting. Making a complete culture change in every area is difficult! Not all were able to do that. Our living conditions were vastly eased by Riz, the company employer who got broken things fixed without waiting weeks, made reservations for air travel, and many other things. Sandra Mackey writes, "Various studies done for Western companies sending large numbers of employees to Saudi

Arabia estimated as many as a third could not cope with the demands of their jobs, an alien culture, and the difficult living conditions."

Many of those families did not have a Riz. Some even had to cook with only a few small gas burners that lay on the floor. At the opposite extreme, we had a friendship with a wealthy Saudi and his American wife. He amused us one evening by showing us the piece of furniture "that I'm refinishing." In actuality, some of their servants were doing the refinishing!

American Holidays

I had plenty of time one Halloween to make our older son a pirate costume using material from two of my dresses. I sewed while I provided company for our younger son, who was confined to bed. He had such a sensitive system that any time he got a cold, it progressed into pneumonia. That occurred eleven times in two years. There was really no treatment possible other than keeping him in bed and giving him some medicine to increase his appetite. He ate a great deal every meal and between meals too! Despite his illness, he was always in good spirits. We were very thankful upon returning to live in the States to have the issue solved through allergy shots.

Arab graciousness came into play when our Egyptian neighbor invited our Lebanese neighbors, our Saudi neighbors, and our family to a turkey dinner for Thanksgiving. We enjoyed a turkey with the Arabic stuffing. It was rice-based instead of bread-based. I really liked the food better than the traditional American Thanksgiving meal. Among other things, we had yellow squash stuffed with rice and hamburger, puff pastry with meat and pinion nuts on top, a dip made with eggplant and tomatoes stuffed with garlic and parsley.

I had only met that Saudi neighbor a couple of times. She was quite emancipated in that she did not veil unless she went to the *Souk*. She was quite a beauty as many of the women were under the veils. We teased each other about our different customs. They eat dinner about 12:00 a.m., go to bed about 2:00 or 3:00 a.m., then sleep some each afternoon. I teased her about eating early. She teased me about being up way past my bedtime.

During our five Christmases there, we cut down desert bushes, spray-painted them and decorate them with snowflakes made of Christmas paper. Local stores catering to expatriates added to the festivities by writing "Merry Christmas" on their windows. Our sons each got a few toys. They enjoyed those toys more than if they had received many.

One year we had a carol sing for people who would not be thinking about Christmas otherwise. After playing bridge and singing carols, we exchanged gifts. People as a whole enjoyed the carols so much that when we had finished, someone suggested singing them again. The few who did not enjoy them either did not sing or purposely sang with loud, out-of-tune voices. One of those couples eventually came to know the Lord in Riyadh just as we had two years earlier.

Another year we went to five Christmas parties, including one hosted by our company at a fancy hotel. At least as fancy as was available! When I looked at the menu, I thought I needed to choose, but the meal included everything: soup, fish, steak, turkey, and dessert! We were careful, even in that expatriate-oriented restaurant, to eat no raw vegetables or fruit because of the danger of cholera. We did enjoy their dips which were scooped up with Pita bread. Both the hummus made from chickpeas and the buba gunauch made from eggplant are much more nutritious than our traditional American sour creamed-based dips.

Some dear friends from church gave me three cans of Spam one Christmas. The husband worked with the U.S. government, which meant they could get pork into the country. It was shipped directly to their business without going through customs. What a great treat! When another friend invited my sons and me to lunch and served Spam it seemed like Heaven!

Our older son with Santa Claus

We debated and then decided to take our toddler son to visit Santa Claus with the other children we knew. It would be fun for him and he might get a present. I told him a number of times, "Santa Claus is pretend." We did not want any confusion in his mind. That he clearly understood the birth of our Lord Jesus Christ was the real meaning of Christmas was very important to us. We also felt it was important not to lie to him. So much for the "fun", I expected him to experience. He howled as he sat on Santa's lap! The fear did not last long. I told him again when we got into our car, "Santa Claus is pretend." He quickly replied, "But Mrs. Claus isn't!" So much for the fun and the lesson! Pretty funny!

Roberta Woodberry, wife of the first resident Pastor in Riyadh, Saudi Arabia, since the time of Mohammed, tells her story of making a Good Friday crown, "Although we spoke many languages and came from many denominations we experienced the hymn 'In Christ there is no East or West...but one great fellowship of love.' But how could we celebrate Good Friday and then Easter? For Good Friday, I cut four branches from a thorn tree to make a crown of thorns. Thus began one of the most moving experiences I've ever had. As I tried to shape the branches, the three-inch-long spikes punctured my gloves, and my fingers began to bleed. And to think a crown like that was pushed onto my Savior's head! I began to feel a small bit of the pain Jesus suffered. Through my tears, I looked up the passage in Matthew 27:29-31: "Then they twisted together a crown of thorns and set it on his head. They put a staff in His right hand and knelt in front of Him and mocked Him, 'Hail King of the Jews!' They spat on Him and took the staff and struck Him on the head again and again, then led Him away to crucify Him."

Roberta also remembers Easter, the most meaningful celebration in the Christian faith, "But how could we celebrate in Saudi Arabia as the Saudi government wouldn't allow us to meet in the auditorium? We found an open space in the desert surrounded by boulders of all different sizes. It was far enough away so we wouldn't be noticed from the road. There it was easy to picture a tomb and a large stone rolled away, just like the first Easter. There was a hush as people came through the boulders then saw the crown of thorns and the grave clothes. It was an amazing service! We sang "Christ the Lord Is Risen Today," "Up from the Grave He Arose," and "He Lives!" as the sun in all its glory came up over the desert. Dudley, (Roberta's) husband, preached on the meaning of the Resurrection. We all rejoiced together! We will never forget that service, hidden in the rocks, out in the desert of Saudi Arabia. And there was more! Our Buddhist neighbor who had come to the service with her family told us afterward, 'I'm a Christian now! I gave my life to Jesus!'

Saudi Holidays

The Saudi holidays were, of course, very different than ours. For *Hajj*, the trip to Mecca is required to feel accepted by *Allah*, the men clip their nails, shave or cut their hair, bathe, discard headgear, and exchange shoes for sandals. The men are garbed in a white seamless garment consisting of two long pieces of white seamless cloth, one wound around the waist and the other around the shoulders.

The women are also draped in white, but the garment covers the entire body. The veil is worn only over their hair. Everyone dresses alike during the pilgrimage, so no one is recognized as having greater social standing or affluence.

Men who have been to Mecca are called "*Hajjis*" (pilgrims) and dye their beards red. They sometimes do not have enough money to return to their nations, so they go from door to door saying "*Ana aspha*" ("I am poor") in hopes of getting enough money to return home.

We once were astonished at the ability of a man to completely change into the typical dress without leaving his seat on the plane. He did it with complete modesty. We saw him at one point in regular garb, and then, at next glance, he was dressed for *Hajj*.

Ka'bah

In fun, a *Hajji* would sometimes call out to an expatriate, "Hey, *Hajji!*" which enabled us to enjoy each other.

Not so much fun was waiting in an airport so crowded the only seating was body to body along the wall. An additional challenge was keeping track of our toddler, who did not understand the need to stay in one place. My husband and I took turns following him. It is amazing how one little child can wear out two parents!

When the pilgrims, often numbering more than two million, visit Mecca, they find the Ka'bah, a stone building that is the most sacred place in the city. Set in the southeast corner of the Ka'bah is the Black Stone, which is believed to have been sent down from heaven in ancient times as a sign to men. Over the centuries, the kisses of countless pilgrims have worn it smooth.

It was exciting to see the buses going through town flying flags of the countries of those headed to Mecca. Many stopped and camped overnight in tents outside town. They brought rugs to finance their way further on the trip. It was all very colorful.

My husband, me and friends with rug from Iran

Ramadan is the other required Muslim holiday. The population did not eat, drink or smoke each day from the time a black thread could be distinguished from a white thread at sunup until a black thread could no longer be distinguished from a white thread after sunset. The cannon fired seven times to notify the population of the sighting of a crescent moon at the beginning of Ramadan. The cannon also fired twice each day, once at sunup and the other at sunset, so people knew when to fast or to break the fast. At the end of Ramadan, the cannon was fired seven times again, announcing the end of Ramadan when a new crescent moon was seen. I did not see how they could last the entire month when they partied all night! They did close their shops to sleep during the afternoon. The Saudis who worked for expatriates had a very difficult time keeping our schedule. My husband said the men at work were "as grouchy as all get out!" I had one of the Saudis at the office write a note to our house boy asking him to clean well but not do any extras like ironing or washing windows until after Ramadan. He seemed to appreciate that very much.

Ramadan was one of the times of the year the government allowed beggars to go door to door. The government frowned on non-Muslims giving money, so I gave some to our neighbor. She would have it to give to anyone who asked. The original intent was everybody fast and give the money saved to the poor. It had deteriorated into all-night partying. I was only somewhat sympathetic (as my) husband often fasted as well due to the difficulty of getting food and drink when he was gone for several days. A friend at work once humorously told him he looked like he was celebrating Ramadan. In his case, it was due to having been awake for hours the night before due to one of our sons being ill.

His close relationship with his Saudi co-workers was apparent as he was invited to break the fast with one of them and his three roommates. They had the traditional meal of barley soup, dates, and small squares of pastry with meat and parsley inside. After eating their fill, they were supposed to pray. That group did not. They ate again about 10:00 p.m. and then ate their big meal about 3:00 a.m.

During the month, almost no work was done. Often expatriates took trips sightseeing in other nations. I was among them!

Travels

During my travels, I collected a wall hanging from each nation we visited. The one from Kenya is a giraffe made of banana leaves. It was very exciting to go over the equator on our way there as the pilot said, "One mile," and then counted down until we crossed.

We went to the hotel from the airport at night. As our son looked out the window at the lush vegetation, he said in a voice that revealed his suspicion, "There's something growin' out there!" He was not used to seeing much growing in the desert! Both our sons very much enjoyed the sticks. We did not have many of those around Riyadh either! We had a special song we sang as we strolled around the hotel grounds:

"Heaven and earth are full of Thee.

Heaven and earth are praising Thee,

O, Lord Most High!"

I have never felt the need to visit Hawaii as I picture it as being much like Kenya.

Many expatriates went on safari in Kenya. A friend had a particularly memorable safari drive in the Amboseli National Park. They arrived at their lodging mid-afternoon and met the driver who was to conduct their twilight safari drive. He was a polite Maasai with a wonderful command of the English language. His driving a Range Rover type vehicle with a moon roof allowed them to actually stand up inside the car to get a close-up as well as a safe, clear view of the animals. As he turned his head to speak to them, his ear lobe brushed across his shoulder. As a child, according to custom, a disc had been placed in his ear with the hole gradually increased in size until his was huge! He had evidently forgotten to wear his "ear ornaments" that day which left him earlobes that reached his shoulder. He tired of that annoyance rather quickly. Finally, he took his ear lobe and hooked it over the top of his ear! Problem solved, now on with the safari!

My family and I went on a safari in Kenya as well. Our driver was very personable. We enjoyed conversing with him as well as seeing the animals. It was sad to me that, although he worked each day showing others the beauty and excitement of his country, his family had never seen the animals. He was unable to give his own family what he daily gave to others. It was the lack of a car that prevented them. We left him money to make it possible for him to rent a car to take his family on safari.

Due to the ages of our sons, it was better to go on a mini safari. I still saw many animals at close range. I even saw a rhinoceros about to charge to protect her little one. The tour driver got us out of there fast!

We also saw some of the Maasai tribe standing along the road, hoping tourists would pay to have a picture taken with them. A number of the Maasai had zebra-skinned drums. Our older son got a chuckle when we were reunited with others from our company in the airport. Seeing one of the women with a zebra-skinned drum, he exclaimed, "I didn't know Mrs. Pollock was a Maasai!"

Our souvenirs included a carved elephant, rhinoceros, and several gazelle. My husband also bought a shirt with a typical African print in bright blue, red, yellow, and green on a beige background. It was definitely special order. After taking my husband's measurements, the tailor cut out the shirt, having made so many he did not need a pattern. It was ready to wear in about 20 minutes. After its first wash, it became mine, having shrunk from its original size.

While there, it was interesting to be with English-speaking nationals and be unable to understand each other due to the use of "nappy" instead of "diaper," "serviette" instead of "napkin," and so on. As I tried to order bottled water, the waiter described the situation as, "You don't understand me, and I don't

Pyramid and Sphinx

understand you, and that is where our difficulty arises." Funny as I look back on it. Frustrating at the time!

When visiting Cairo, Egypt, we were able to see the Pyramids at Giza and the Sphinx. It was interesting to see the most recent of the group, the Steppe pyramid, was very poorly made. The technique had been lost. In one of the pyramids, we saw archeologists x-ray, hoping to discover other tombs similar to that which held the riches of King Tut. Afterward, our sons entertained themselves by pretending to be a pyramid and Sphinx.

We saw the King Tut exhibit in a dark, dingy museum. The only light came from windows at the top of the walls and spotlights on each of the exhibits. I realized that explaining what we saw to our sons added a dimension to my visit.

Touring Cairo with a taxi driver who turned off his car at every stoplight to save gas added to memories. He took us to a place where I bought perfume which, according to him, was hundreds of years old. Do you think that might have been a scam? If so, I fell for it! I still have the perfume.

We encountered a problem while in Cairo when a mix-up left us without a hotel reservation for a day and night. While my husband worked out the difficulty with the desk clerk, I entertained our sons by suggesting we sing songs we knew from our church, including

"Isn't He wonderful, wonderful, wonderful? Isn't Jesus my Lord wonderful?

Eyes have seen, Ears have heard, it's recorded in God's Word.

Isn't Jesus my Lord wonderful?!"

We even made up our own verses such as "Didn't He heal the sick..." "Didn't He raise the dead...?" So we were encouraged as we waited. And the Lord provided a wonderful solution. Egyptian relatives of a man with whom my husband worked in Saudi Arabia invited us to stay in their home while they went to stay with relatives. They even stocked the refrigerator!

A worse problem was my getting so sick while there, I had

to call to my husband, knowing I could not make it from the bathroom back to bed on my own. Fortunately, there was a hotel doctor to help me. What a way to spend Christmas! My husband took our sons to the gift shop in the motel. They chose pyramid-shaped stones made of quartz which have now been given to their children.

My Mom was a record keeper and that proved to be of great benefit. The doctor at the hotel in Egypt suggested I begin to drink coffee and salt everything I ate to raise my blood pressure. I began that practice once back in Riyadh and had great times drinking coffee with my younger sister, who was visiting from Australia. After the month-long round trip, a letter to my parents in the States required, I learned the blood pressure the doctor saw was perfectly normal for me. I stopped drinking coffee as I did not like the taste and had to add a great deal of sugar to make it palatable to me.

Switzerland was one of our favorite destinations. It was so clean! And everything was run on a strict time schedule. Both of which were a contrast to Saudi Arabia. In Interlaken, Switzerland, we toured a cave in Jungfrau Mountain, which contained ice sculptures. Our children had no winter coats as they were not needed in Saudi Arabia. We had them put on all the shirts I had packed as well as the green corduroy coats their Grandmother had made. My husband kept them entertained while we waited for our tour bus by making up a song, "I cannot walk. I cannot walk to the station, for I'm frozen to death. Can't you see my cold breath?!" We also took a train ride through part of the country. At times we would pass through a tunnel. I would jokingly say to our sons, "How do you think you're going to like living in the center of the earth?" We very much enjoyed seeing the cattle with their bells. It visualized Heidi by Johanna Spyri for me.

Beirut, Lebanon, was an oasis for us even though the driving had dangerous aspects. Drivers would pass on a blind curve as we rode through the mountainous terrain. One driver told us he would win playing "chicken" with any taxi driver in New York City!

We toured many different places there, including an underground river. As we exited, those waiting to enter patted our sons on the heads as they passed. The Arab people like children. Ours being blond was an additional attraction.

We also visited nearby Byblos, the site of the longest inhabited city in the world. The guide showed us the remaining parts of dwellings people had made when they came from caves to live. There were also remains from a Crusader castle. It was interesting to me to learn the word "Bible" came from the word "Byblos." The first writing was on parchment from there.

With Beirut as our starting point because of airline connections, we saw many sights. Italy where we heard they did not like children, but where our waiter acted out the various kinds of sandwiches so we would know what to order. He more than compensated for our not knowing Italian and made it much more fun! England where we visited Buckingham Palace, Westminster Abbey where Robert Browning, Geoffrey Chaucer, Robert Browning, Charles Dickens, and Rudyard Kipling and others are buried, Madam Tussaud's Wax Museum and a park where our sons enjoyed the squirrels more than the animals at the zoo we had visited earlier! Holland, where we saw cheese made and enjoyed gorgeous tulips. My favorite part of that visit was going to the small island just off Amsterdam, where tourists were given a map of the island on one side of the paper and a map to Heaven through the death and resurrection of Jesus Christ on the other. Munich, Germany, where we sat in the main square and our children creatively entertained each other and amused us. They pretended they were rhinoceroses by putting two straws on the appropriate places on their faces then used the straws for a sword fight. Paris, France, where we saw painters at Montmartre art colony. While there, our older son wheeled the younger in his stroller much faster than the younger thought safe. I can still picture him covering his eyes with his hands, so he did not need to look at what seemed a near disaster! Copenhagen, Denmark, where we saw workers excavating a Viking ship. While there, we also saw the harbor with the statue of the Little Mermaid from the book by Hans Christian Anderson. Upon seeing a statue of a child urinating, our younger son did not say a word but assumed the pose, with his clothes on, of course. Hilarious! And Paphos, Cyprus, where we saw the stone to which the Apostle Paul was tied then beaten.

Cyprus was also the site of our most frightening trip. We had finished our shopping and were returning to the hotel when my husband heard shots. As we hurried along, some people motioned us to come into their home. It was complete with a machine gun sitting on the dining room table! When my husband decided to try to get back to the hotel, each of us carried a son and ran. He told me later the bullets were so close he could hear them ricocheting! We stayed in our hotel for four days. Our sons and I spent hours sitting on the bed singing Christian songs. The four-year-old told his two-year-old brother to "say it after me," giving him words to ask Jesus to be his Savior. Our younger son would do anything his brother told him to do but did not really have the understanding necessary to receive Christ. It touched me to see our older son's spiritual concern for his brother. When a cease-fire was announced, we were able to make it to the airport, where a special Middle East Airlines plane came to evacuate us. I was very pleased with our sons as they shared the toys and books they had with other children. When we saw the airplane landing, our toddler son ran to the huge window calling out, "Here I am, MEA! Here I am!" My husband caused the deplaning newsmen concern by motioning and saying, "Go back! Go back!" but then let them know he was teasing. There was some danger as my husband collected tank shells from the roof of our hotel!

Before one of those trips, I decided to let our younger son keep his bottle even though he was at an age where he could very easily begin to use a cup. It was an easy way to carry water. In some of the countries we visited, drinking tap water was not safe. His older brother could take the top off to drink, and he would use the nipple. When we returned home, I used a weaning method that was supposed to be foolproof. Just cut the bottom off the bottle and show the child that it no longer worked. Our son had a solution, though. "Use Scotch Tape." He was a great problem solver!

We had hoped to visit Israel when we returned to the States permanently, but just before we left Saudi Arabia, a farmer ran over my husband's foot with a Ditch Witch. Since it was broken, it seemed best to get home as soon as possible. Our dear doctor friend from church had my husband sit on the bidet in our bathroom while he put a cast on it. That was the only time we ever used the bidet!

Contrasts within Riyadh

It felt great to be safely home. Riz, the Ford Foundation employee who took care of us, hired someone to clean our villa. It was in better shape than when we left! That never happened in the States! Riyadh was home. It was good to have returned even though it was a curiosity to us expatriates.

As a city of more than 300,000 people, it had a great contrast within itself. It was oil wealth and desert-dwelling poverty. It was modern paved streets without names and it was vacant lots where you picked your own trail and tried to avoid the ruts. It was concrete buildings and mud buildings. It was palaces and shacks made of tin and scrap lumber. It was jewelry stores on the main street and hundreds of one-room stores made of cinder blocks and mud in the *Souk*. It was mixed gatherings of internationals and separation of men from women so great my husband could not go with me to an open house at our son's expatriate school.

Medically it was a doctor from Lebanon performing surgery on a female friend with a ruptured appendix and it was male doctors unable a see female patients. It was a doctor having a metal tongue depressor which he put into alcohol between most patients. The expatriates each got his/her own stick. Our dear Lebanese doctor friend came out during the night by taxi to see our younger son, who had croup. A doctor inoculated one of our sons with glass from the broken vile he had put on the floor. It was an eye, ear, nose, and throat specialist doing brain surgery when a child fell into an empty swimming pool and preserved his life. It was the humorous situation of our older son holding his breath and repeatedly gasping as he waited for an x-ray. I had told him the doctor would ask him to hold his breath. "What's wrong?!" the doctor asked, thinking our son was having a seizure of some type. It was getting laughs from the technicians at the hospital when our son exclaimed "a-ee, a-aa!" over and over as he did not want to cry when he was inoculated. It was the same son telling a doctor "*moffie stick*" ("no stick") as he did not like the tongue depressor and thought the Arabic word for "no" was more easily understood! Sadly it was sometimes treatment without anesthesia. When our younger son needed stitches in his forehead as a result of hitting his head on the bookshelf, the physician just told me, "Hold him. Pin his arms down while I stitch him up." A hard thing for both mother and son! Fortunately, Riz was at home at the time of the accident and available to take us to the hospital as my husband was out of town. I was VERY thankful to have a telephone as most people did not.

Contrasts to the United States

Riyadh certainly was a contrast to my former life in the States. In fact, one friend described the contrast by saying, "Do you ever feel like Saudi Arabia is another part of Disney Land when you are in the States and the States is another part of Disney Land when you are in Saudi Arabia. Each location required one's full attention.

I noticed the difference in climate the minute I stepped off the airplane. It felt like all the liquid was being sucked out of my body. There is a vast difference in the average October temperatures in Longmont, Colorado, of 67/38 and in Riyadh average of 94/67. Rainfall was vastly different as well, with approximately 15 ½ inches per year in Longmont and approximately 2 ½ inches of rain per year in Riyadh. Although at times, Colorado farmers desire more rainfall, there is not the dire need for rain that often exists in Saudi Arabia. Most of the water used there comes from underground reservoirs, which are a nonrenewable resource. Some believe the water will run out before the oil in that nation. Scientists are working to make desalting ocean water economically feasible.

Undoubtedly the most important contrast is the spiritual practices of the two beliefs. Islam is a religion of law. Christianity is a religion of grace. Muslims believe they must, by their own efforts, do certain works to attain favor with *Allah*. They continually try to reach up to God. Christians believe God reached down to us through Jesus Christ, His perfect Son. All that is needed is to trust in Him. He then gives us the power to live in a way that is pleasing to Him.

Muslims are ruled by *Sharia* law. They believe Jesus was a great prophet but Mohammed was the last, and therefore the greatest, prophet. Neither do they believe in the Trinity. As is stated in the Koran: "Allah is one Allah: Glory be to Him (far exalted is He) above having a son." Christians believe in the eternally relational Creator God the Father, the Son, and the Holy Spirit.

They worship by bowing down in the direction of Mecca five times a day. Many mornings prayer starts at 4:30. During the day, metal shutters clang down over storefronts, and the men crowd around the long rows of water spigots to perform their ablutions—the washing of the face, nostrils, ears, hands, and feet before praying.

That is one of the five pillars of faith and is known as the *Salat*. The other pillars are *Shahada* (profession of faith—there is no god but *Allah* and Mohammed is his prophet), *Zakat* (alms giving), *Sawm* (fasting), and *Hajj* (pilgrimage). Often one would see them with their prayer beads similar to rosary beads counting off prayers as they stood on corners or went about their business.

They believe at the end of a person's life, *Allah* weighs good and bad deeds. Having the good outweigh the bad does not necessarily mean entrance into Paradise. That is something *Allah* randomly decides. A man who is able to enter Paradise is surrounded by many virgins. The single guaranteed way to attain Paradise is to be killed in *jihad* (religious war). This may explain situations such as that which occurred in the States on 9/11.

Theirs is a Fear/Power framework causing them to focus on appeasing evil spirits, Guilt/Innocence causing them to focus on right and wrong and Shame/ Honor causing them to focus on saving face for the sake of self and community.

The Shame/Honor framework explains the story we heard about a family with an unmarried, pregnant daughter. After leaving Saudi Arabia to give birth to the baby in Beirut, Lebanon, her family lured her back into the country. Then they killed her because she brought dishonor to their family.

A happier story is of a princess who went to Beirut to have an out-of-wedlock baby. The baby girl was adopted by our good friends there. That baby was about six years old when we moved to Saudi Arabia. She gave our children the books she had outgrown. Her Mom was the one mentioned earlier who made a pork roast each time we visited them.

In the Muslim culture, the whole is more important than the individual. It is essential to fit into the community. When a family is shamed by an individual, he may not be welcome any longer in the mosque. A person's brothers and sisters may not be able to find suitable marriages. The family business may suffer. This means some young men when becoming Christians, feel they must be secret believers since they are dependent on their families for the necessities of life. They would be declared dead to the family because of the shame they brought if it were known they followed Jesus.

Ours is a Right/Wrong framework now tending toward Pleasure/Pain: "If it feels good, do it." and "What is right for you is not necessarily right for me."

One similarity between the two religions is the people of both believe Jesus will return to the earth, but beliefs about His return differ greatly. Muslims believe Jesus will return as a Muslim and will "break the cross and kill the pigs" (*Sahih Bukhari*, Volume 3 Book 43, Number 656). He will live for forty years during which He will marry, have children, and perform *Hajj*. After his death, He will be buried beside the grave of the Prophet Mohammed. (*Sahih Bukhari*, Volume 9, Book 88, Number 242). Christians believe His second coming will be universally visible and so dramatic no one will fail to recognize Him (Matthew 24:30). Philippians 2:11 states when He comes, "every knee shall bow, every tongue confess that He is LORD." Revelations 23 states He is coming for those who are His through believing He died on the cross and rose again and that He will establish the new heaven and new earth.

A much less important difference is the homes in which I've lived. My new home was very different from the one in Colorado. The villa in Riyadh was surrounded by an eight-foot wall to prevent men from seeing me, or my husband from seeing our neighbors' wives or daughters. I once called over to our Canadian neighbor, "I hope you can't see our son. He doesn't have his diaper on."

He called back, "I hope you can't see me. I don't have mine on either!"

The roof of our villa was flat, which provided me a place to hang the wash. Our roof also was used for our sons' birthday parties. It was a great play area!

And the voltage was different as well. Actually, it was not the voltage. Both were 110, but the frequency was different. In the States, it was 50, and in Saudi Arabia, it was 60. I learned that in an alarming way. Plugging in our phone brought from the State resulted in it ringing madly and then dying. I learned my lesson and always used an adaptor when I ironed.

In the States, there was no danger of losing your home as long as you paid the rent or mortgage. The same was not true in Riyadh. As prices for rent keep increasing, the government tried to bring it to a stop by stating there could be only a limited increase. The resident could not be evicted in order to charge more to the new renter, often a business. The only loophole was residents could be put out if the owner's relative intended to move there. One day we got the dreaded phone call. But there was a reprieve when the English-speaking son met with us, saying he had convinced his mother to let us stay. Sometime after, there came another call which resulted in our move. The Lord had shown me His power in keeping the villa for us. I could also trust He was in control when we did not get to keep our villa. Later I decided to call our former phone number. As I expected a secretary answered the phone for the company that had rented it. But the Lord says in the Bible in Romans 8:28, "And we know all things work together for good to them that love God, to them who are the called according to His purpose." In this case, the good came from us moving into an apartment building in which our sons had a friend to play with for the first time. Even if it was sometimes with Barbies!

Airports were vastly different from those to which we were accustomed. At one time, the airport in Riyadh was located in a Quonset hut. Ours in Denver was highly organized with plenty of room. Theirs sometimes were so crowded we had to carry our sons to keep one or the other from being stepped on. It made waiting in the airport a grim experience.

And the baggage system! Again order versus disorder. In Saudi Arabia, a man would run up to slap the trunk of your vehicle, indicating he would be the one to carry your luggage and receive the tip. My husband humorously commented, referring to the book *Texas* by Michener, "They are counting coupe."

Sandra Mackey described the scene inside: "baggage handlers of a dozen different nationalities, speaking a dozen different languages, were tossing luggage off an antiquated conveyor belt into a makeshift holding pen. Passengers missed their bags as they flew by, yelling at the handlers while climbing over the barricades in a frantic effort to retrieve their suitcases. Others who had arrived days earlier wandered through the mountains of unclaimed baggage in an odyssey of despair, searching for their lost possessions...Even the ever-polite British, the originators and vigilant defenders of the queue, were pushing and shouting as they tried to get through the mob with their suitcases.

There was also a contrast in the age at which the population began to work. Young people did not work until their teens in the States. Some preteens in Saudi Arabia had the heavy responsibility of tending their younger siblings plus sheep and goats. They moved the goats from place to place, locating food and water. We saw that goats really do eat paper!

The "separating the sheep from the goats" passage in the Bible (Matthew 25:32) became more meaningful as Saudi sheep and goats were much more alike in appearance than they were in the States. Both had long, shaggy hair and both varied in color. The clue to distinguishing was the sheep's tails went down and the goats' went up.

Woman in the center offered me her ring

Another difference was in the attitude toward material possessions. A popular bumper sticker in the States read, "He who dies with the most toys wins!" In contrast, a Saudi store clerk told my husband, "I'm not going to order any more of that bowl. Everyone wants to buy it. Then I have to order more!"

One man in their culture was very highly thought of because he gave away all he owned. Bedouins felt anybody who came to their tents should be fed whether or not they had enough for themselves. I encountered something a bit similar when I admired a friend's unusual gold ring. She started to take it off to give it to me!

Giving was also seen in the story a Canadian friend told about a Saudi with whom he worked. The Saudi announced he was going to have a party at the Canadian's home. Since the Saudi had been invited to the Canadian's home, the proverb, "My house is your house," came into play. The man felt he could invite others since he himself had been invited. The Canadian was rescued by a Lebanese man who said, "The house is really too small. You should have the party somewhere else."

In the States, I lived in a society was very conscious of time. I had a clock in many rooms of my home. In Saudi Arabia, time meant very little. Society ran on getting things done *"bucra"* ("tomorrow"). If someone said something would be done *"bucra"* it was usually done eventually. One better not get one's hopes set on something happening when a Saudi said, *"bucra enshala"* ("tomorrow if God wills.") An expatriate joke stated, *"'Bucra enshala"* is like *"manana"* in Spanish but without the sense of urgency!

The difference in the penal system horrified the expatriates. Punishments each Friday at Punishment Square included chopping off the right hand for stealing and sometimes a beheading. The Saudi justice system was truly "an eye for an eye and a tooth for a tooth" as the person convicted of harming his neighbor was punished by the same act he had committed. If the crime had been murder, the blindfolded criminal, his hands tied behind his back, would drop his head forward while the executioner unsheathed his sword then swung it down until metal met flesh. When the thief who stole a friend's car was captured, it was expected he would have his hand cut off. Saudis would probably point to their low crime rate as compared to the rate in our country where trials drag on for weeks, appeals for years, and often criminals are released after completing only part of their prison sentences.

Another contrast, there was never the possibility we would need to prepare for a war in the States. After my husband returned from a trip to inspect the farms, we discussed things that happened while we were apart. Just before falling asleep that night, I suddenly remembered, "I forgot to tell you. There is a war!"

And he replied, "I forgot to tell you!" The Israelis and Arabs had been fighting for two days. We had just heard about it!

As a general rule, we never worried about the news as we did not get a newspaper until everything was over. The news did make some impression on our older son as he once pretended he was an airplane pilot named Nixon!

Since the war situation was a serious one, my husband drew a map to our villa for the embassy in case evacuation was necessary. We also prepared a list of what to take if needed. We felt we were in no danger but we would be deported if the U.S. supplied weapons to Israel. Knowing the mail was censored, we were careful what we wrote to our families. The States being pro-Israel caused us some embarrassment when with our Arab friends, but most of them accepted us as individuals, not as Americans supporting their enemy. There was very little censored from the Paris newspaper, but since it was about eight days late, we had to depend on short radio broadcasts during that time.

An interesting view of the Saudis toward their nation can be stated as "I against my brothers; I and my brothers against my cousins; I and my cousins against the world." As Americans, we were part of "the world." We needed to be ready to exit the country if needed. King Faisal was forced to bend to the hardline Arab forces in the Arab-Israeli dispute, which conflicted with the monarchy's need to maintain its relationship with the United States.

A fastidious homemaker in the States would have been horrified at finding weevils in a bag of flour just purchased from the grocery store. In Riyadh, I remember talking with a neighbor as she sifted them out of her bag. Neither of us was embarrassed. It was just a fact of life. After all, we were careful to freeze them, so they were dead before we sifted the flour! The descriptive phrase was *molish* ("It does not matter").

It was not *molish* to see the twenty or thirty flies around our younger son's mouth until he was old enough to learn to shoo them away or to have many ants in our villa bringing in sand to build their homes. My husband took a picture of a huge group of them actually carrying a Frito chip up the wall!

Having the "Riyadh Runs" was not *molish* either. Kaopectate was my friend! I was so sick one time I just laid on the floor by the toilet, knowing I did not have the energy to get back to bed and then to the bathroom again. Our tender-hearted toddler son pulled a pillow off the bed and laid it by my head.

We learned to accept the absence of water pressure as *molish*. Instead of the pressure to which we are accustomed in the States, water was pumped up to the metal tank on the roof from an underground tank. The water then flowed from the faucets through the pull of gravity. Most of the year, Riyadh was so hot the water which came from the metal tank needed to be cooled. We used the water in the hot water heater for that purpose.

When the city was not able to supply all the water needed, we would order a diesel truck to supply it. I became one of the first recyclers by using dishwater to water plants in our yard. I did waste some water when I let our sons wash dishes as a form of entertainment. I could not stand to watch even though it was great fun for them. I just left the room and let them go at it! When I did have to order water, it was fun for our sons to play in the water from the huge hose as there was always more than the tank would hold.

The water which came through city lines was undrinkable as there was a danger of cholera since sewage water was sometimes sucked in through holes in the pipes. The Pepsi factory was our source of drinking water. You might be able to guess what our sons' favorite drink was when we would visit relatives in the States. Tap water! It is amusing that whatever is hard to get becomes a treat!

An unpleasant contrast between our two nations was having frequent inoculations overseas. Our older son developed a phobia about Band-Aids from associating them with needles. He would cry and start yelling, "No Band-Aid! No Band-aid!" Eventually, he and his brother chose to watch when an inoculation was given. It probably made them feel more in control.

The use of alcohol was another contrast. No liquor was allowed into the country, but on occasion, a man would come to our door asking if we wanted to buy *sedeeqi* ("my friend"). He evidently thought all expatriates would want to buy liquor. Occasionally an expatriate was caught making alcohol. Most went to jail, but in 1978 a furor erupted when two British nationals were publically flogged for selling *sedeeqi.*

And can you imagine your husband taking another wife?! That is as common in Saudi Arabia as seeing the wives riding in the back of a Toyota pickup. A humorous situation occurred when a friend took his wife and me to get inoculations. A Saudi asked, "Two wives?!" Our friend replied with a straight face: "Yes." The same friend was once offered a camel for his wife as she had red hair!

The difference in driving was hilarious! We heard of an accident caused by a Saudi running a red light. The policeman thought it over and said to the American, "It's your fault. You can drive and he can't." We also heard of a situation where the American was declared guilty in a traffic accident even though he was nowhere near his car. The reason given, "If the car hadn't been parked along the curb, the accident wouldn't have happened!" Passengers riding in a taxi involved in a wreck were responsible for the accident because if the passenger had not hired the taxi, it would not have been where the accident occurred.

We were sent some traffic instructions stating, "He must not drive reverse in busy traffic streets" and noticed a person could be fined 55 Saudi piasters or four days imprisonment for "not stopping the horn when the camels are stampeding."

I actually did not see camels in town often, although a Bedouin relative of a neighbor rode one in from the desert. I took a picture of my husband sitting on it to send to his Dad for Father's Day. The next day they slaughtered it and left the head, legs, and entrails in the vacant lot between our villas. No wonder there were so many flies!

I could have sent a picture of a typical Riyadh traffic jam as well. Crossing busy streets was a matter of forging ahead, leaning on the horn and the driver with the most guts making it across first. Sometimes there were so many cars in the intersection it was impossible for anyone to move. One of the men would then climb out of his car and direct the traffic until it was untangled. One day I saw a driver turn left from the middle lane on a red light. I was not even very shocked.

And they did love their horns which played "She'll Be Comin' Round the Mountain" or a similar Western melody. The horn was used to warn a driver who was driving in both lanes to move over when one wanted to pass. A horn was also needed to indicate a green light as the first driver in line pulled too far into the intersection to see what color the light was. When our horn was out of operation for a period of time, I felt very unsafe as driving was dependent on it.

The driving was so atrocious my husband said he never failed to see an accident on his way home from work. One day he told me about an Italian man whose car had broken down, so he stopped to help. The man did not speak English, and he did not speak Italian, so they conversed in the little bit of Arabic each knew. Pretty funny!

Clicking the tongue, the way Saudis expressed disbelief, occurred during a class taught by Saudis who had been in the States for those who would be going. When told, "Men should not hold hands," the whole audience started clicking their tongues. That was another difference in culture.

A far-reaching difference was that people, not machines, moved heavy objects. Most of the lifting and carrying was done by men from Yemen, even though they were small in stature. We once saw a Yemeni carrying a refrigerator on his back down the street. Another carried a bag of concrete up a ladder for a villa being built in our neighborhood.

When our company plumber/electrician came to fix something, he had his Yemeni handyman do all the heavy, dirty work. He did not so much as open a door for him.

The plumber/electrician also drove a Toyota pickup to bring the Yemeni, who collected the garbage and trash from all the company homes. The Yemeni did all the work while he sat in the pickup. And he did not let the Yemeni sit in the cab. The plumber/electrician had him sit in the back with the garbage sacks! Maybe you would have to be in the culture to think that funny. Part of the humor was in realizing that the men doing all the work would feel very uncomfortable if the one higher on the job scale suddenly began to help.

We helped prepare a group of Saudis for culture shock in a small way when we hosted them before they left to become students in the States. Among other things, they wanted to know if it would be possible to live on the salary the government would be paying them. They also wanted to know how to dress their children. Would it be cheaper to buy clothes in Riyadh or in the States? Many questions were asked and answered. I had asked the same type of questions as we prepared for our move to Saudi Arabia. I especially wondered about the availability of shoes and decided to take a pair in each size. We thoroughly enjoyed our time with the students. They had a camera and tripod and commemorated the time by taking a group picture.

Relationships

Younger son mimicking the older

Our sons' relationship was a very close one, with the younger often mimicking the older. Also involved was a pecking order. It was our sons' custom to have the older one look at the whole pile of books while his little brother waited for his turn. And he never heard nursery rhythms as his older brother had as, when he typically would have listened to them, he was listening to chapter books, his brother's favorites. Do you think that might have contributed to his intelligence?

Their love of books resulted in our older son's teaching himself to read at age 3. He asked me to point to the words as I read to him. After a period of time, I decided to help him learn to read. I took a book from the Dr. Seuss series and began to instruct. But he did not need instruction. He began to read the book to me! Fortunately, I had purchased many early reading books at a garage sale just before we left the States, so he had many books to read to his brother.

The older also used each crayon before the younger. The younger did have an advantage in that he learned everything his brother was learning. An example was the names of the colors of crayons in their 48 Crayola box. It was amusing. He did not know what the color was, but he did know what it was NOT. He got quite frustrated if we called "Thistle" "purple"!

Our younger son did have some things all his own. He played with approximately 50 small plastic animals almost daily, sometimes lining them up according to color, sometimes according to size, sometimes according to whether they were farm or zoo animals.

His first kindergarten class was in a school near his grandparents' home in Colorado. Then it was on to Houston, Texas, when his Dad took a position with the National Aeronautical and Space Administration. I was surprised when he was chosen to go to still another kindergarten class when the number of students resulted in the class being split into two. He must have been seen as a very stable, secure little child to have been chosen for that unnecessary change.

And his entrance into kindergarten when we moved back to the States revealed the quality of the education his brother gave. One of his kindergarten teachers asked each of the children to count. After counting far enough the teacher stopped him, he told her, "I can count further than that, but sometimes it hurts my throat. At one time, he and his brother decided to see if they could count to 1,000. They could!

There was plenty of time to look, to color, or to look up books or to line up animals as there were not the many away-from-home activities that are the norm for children growing up in the States.

As a result of much time together, our sons were so close sometimes when I walked somewhere with one while the other was with his Dad, the one with me would keep turning around, expecting his brother to be there. They had a deep love for each other.

They liked to play Snow White and the Seven Dwarfs, each wearing a coat with a hood. The older had an advantage in that his coat was not as heavy as his brother's. That was quite an advantage in the heat of Saudi Arabia!

Some of their play involved animals. They had a Smokey the Bear record which said, "When in danger, climb a tree." I would sometimes change it to "When in danger climb a Mom, much to their amusement." They also had a Bambi record and would sometimes play deer and hunter with their Dad. One time our older son got so deeply involved in the play he jumped into my lap, saying, "I thought you were dead! I thought you were dead!" He thought the hunter had killed me.

I told him, "I was in the thicket all the time," to help him transition from play to reality.

At times our younger son did stick up for himself. For instance, one time playing on our flat roof, the older said to him, "Let's pretend the one in the red shirt always wins" (the races). The younger thought a moment and then replied, "Let's not pretend that."

Each of them defended the other. On a visit to school, our preschool son started a fight with an older child he thought was not speaking respectfully to his brother. And his brother defended him at an early age when we were on vacation. We were trying to quiet his singing as we were all sleeping in the same room. "Don't boooother him. He's happy," was his older brother's admonition to us.

Their closeness was partially due to the fact they had a good number of years where they had only each other as playmates. Those years of bonding brought wonderful results as they grew older. One of their close friends in high school said he had never seen them argue. Each was best man at his brother's wedding.

They had a great deal of fun growing up. I remember one afternoon sending them outside to eat a snack. I did not want to invite ants into our home. When I heard them laughing, I looked out the window. Everything seemed to be fine. It was only when our younger son needed to blow his nose before his nap I saw what had caused the laughter. He blew out piece after piece of watermelon! It surprised me as he was so fastidious that he once requested a napkin and a fork to make a table on the seat of his tricycle when I sent them outside with pieces of cake.

Humor

Our children provided us with many laughs. When we first arrived in Riyadh, our older son was 2 ½ years old and the younger three months old. When we would see a truck driver prostrating in prayer (What a contrast to the loose way God is sometimes treated in our culture!) on the side of the road or witnessed another cultural difference, we explained, "Mohammed taught them to do that." It was an easily understood, true explanation. One day I told our older son that when I was in the bathroom, the door should be closed if our house boy was in the house. Men should not see women in the bathroom. His response: "Is that what Mohammad taught them?"

There were many other humorous situations as well. Our younger son, who could not yet read, had memorized the names of the authors. Then he could play that game of Authors with his brother and me. Upon seeing a man at our company swimming pool with what was not a typical Saudi appearance, he said in a shocked voice, "He looks just like Alfred Lord Tennyson!"

One day after school, his brother told me, "There are two boys who don't speak any English, but they are trying very hard to learn—they speak British." It turned out to be Swedish!

At Thanksgiving time, when our older son was studying about the Pilgrims and Indians in kindergarten, he asked, "Did there really used to be white people?"

Another time when a woman brought her toddler over for our house boy's care, I forgot to tell our sons he would be there when they returned from school. They greeted me with excitement. Both had huge smiles as one told me, "I didn't know we were expecting a baby!"

When we hung a picture of Christ over the dinette table, our younger thought it was a picture of Ali Baba as we were reading *The Arabian Knights* aloud.

On a small airplane flying back to Riyadh, we let our older son walk to the back for exercise. When he returned, the Saudi man following him humorously told us, "First, he asked my daughter how old she was. Then he asked her how many teeth she had. Does he think he's buying a horse?!"

It was nearly impossible to get tender meat. As he learned to talk, our younger son thought the word for "meat" was "tough." We said, "This is tough!" often as we ate it. It was imported from Australia, where the cattle ran wild and had cactus and tree bark to eat. No wonder it was tough! We learned to eat mostly ground meat, chicken, or shrimp.

My husband encountered some humorous situations at work. A colloquial word for "down" was "dammit." Originally the Saudis only knew the word for "up." They would shout it during their work for the American Arabian Oil Company whether it was up or down. When the worker would start hauling up when they wanted down, the boss would yell, "Dammit!" and gesture down. They picked it up!

We did our best housing our school. That meant meeting in a house with a huge bathroom that held the ditto machine and featured an eye chart over the bathtub. A little girl needing to go to the toilet asked, "Where's the bathtub?"

We did not think our son would receive a nickname when we named him Craig. But young children are very creative. He soon was stuck with "Craig Egg." When his cousin in the States heard about the nickname, she thought it was pretty neat. "Maybe the kids will call me Jessica Egg." It was fitting she admired him. When he learned she had been born, he was so excited! He went running out of our villa yelling, "We can call her Dressy Betsy," the name of a doll at that time.

In another humorous situation, our friends told of seeing an engraved copper plate of the Lord's Supper in the *Souk*. The shopkeeper told him, "That's the second dinner."

Souk

The *Souk* was a honeycomb of 30 to 40 thousand shops with those selling the same items clustered together along a dirt path. Most of the shops were small enough the owner could sit in the center and reach most of his merchandise.

Saudi women did not often frequent the *Souk*. They stayed almost completely at home or in each other's homes. We would see probably 100 men shopping for each woman seen. Even princesses rarely left the palace. There were many as King Abdul-Aziz, the first monarch of Saudi Arabia, had 45 sons and about 30 daughters.

We expatriates did not want to stay home, and going to the *Souk* (the least expensive, most conservative shopping area in Riyadh) was one of our favorite forms of entertainment.

The Gold *Souk* was particularly intriguing as stacks of 18 and 21 karat gold bangle bracelets and other jewelry were stacked in what was really more like a hovel than a shop. It was not unusual to see an African maid wearing many of those gold bracelets and necklaces. It was their banking system.

Veiled women sat on the ground outside some of the shops selling various types of edible seeds. It was easy to get lost on the path that wound along the shops. A friend and I did get lost once but, after praying, we saw our husbands coming toward us. What a relief!

Taking with you an item similar to what you wanted to purchase was a great aid. When we used the expression "*acula wahad*" ("same one"), the shopkeeper knew what to show us. Or they would use the expression "same, same" as they sought to convince us what they had was equal in quality as what we showed

Author in thob on Halloween

them. And the word would spread. As we walked along the path, other shopkeepers would come out with their similar merchandise.

We wore *thobs* like those worn by the Saudi men but made of colorful materials. Obviously, we did not want an owner in a *thob* shop taking pleasure in measuring us. Each new arrival was taken to a *thob*-maker who already had measurements of someone her size. I still have my *thob* and wear it each year when our church has its annual Fall Festival on Oct. 31.

One time a friend was in the Souk. She had her head covered with a scarf. The *matawa* (religious policeman) told her to veil (cover her whole face as the Saudi women do). She pulled the scarf over her face and her husband led her around. I found that pretty funny!

What was not funny was a *matawa* sometimes used his stick to hit a woman on the leg if he thought she should be dressing more conservatively.

Our Kuwaiti chest

The *Souk* was a great place to buy Swiss watches and quality cameras at a much lower price than we would have paid in the States. Both my husband and I bought Omega watches. There was a downside, though. The shopkeeper said the guarantee was for "one time around!"

Most expatriates purchased Kuwaiti chests. They were boxes made of various exotic woods, which sailors decorated on long sea trips made to Australia and other nations to purchase products such as meat to be sold in the stores in Kuwait. Thus the name. Ours is mahogany decorated with beautifully carved wood on the front and brass nails laid in a geometric pattern on the top. My husband and I took turns deciding what purchases to make. After I chose the Kuwaiti chest, he chose the painting of a Saudi street in the old part of town, mud buildings on either side. He tells people it is very accurate except it needs to have goats eating garbage! It was easy for us to spend money. First, we were being paid very well to work there, and second, riyals, the Saudi bills, seemed like Monopoly money, not cold hard cash! And after all, there were four riyals to an American dollar!

Bargaining was very much part of the shopping process. The seller would expound on the attributes of the item while the potential buyer pointed out the defects. Both the seller and the buyer started at a flexible price and arrived at a price somewhere in the middle, which suited both. I felt very proud of being able to use the system when I got a storekeeper to go from fifteen riyals to twelve for a toy guitar for our older son. Over time a number of newly arrived expatriates did not recognize the need for bargaining. This presented a hardship for the Saudis as the storekeepers began to refuse to bargain even with their fellow citizens. Part of bargaining was to ask for "*bucksheesh*" ("a little for nothing"), which meant we always got a little extra fabric or a vegetable free when shopping. I remember getting a turnip *bucksheesh* one time. It is interesting what a person's mind remembers over many years!

The shopkeepers liked little children, and ours, being blond, received extra attention. One time when shopping in the *Souk*, I suddenly realized our preschool son was gone! I stayed in the store, hoping he would return. My friend set out to find him. As she looked, each shopkeeper stood in his doorway, pointing the direction he had taken. She found him completely lost and turning around in circles in the Gold *Souk*. When we were reunited, I gave him a couple of swats and then hugged and hugged him. A friend later asked me, "Did the storekeeper say "*Harram!*" ("Forbidden")? They did not think it was proper to discipline young children. A few stores down the way, as a man was showing me some material, our son started walking across it as it lay on the floor. I said, "Oh, don't do that!" The shopkeeper said, "No! No!" He probably thought I was going to spank him again and was trying to protect him.

Interactions

In a more positive interaction, a shopkeeper with a very expensive rug in front of his shop thoroughly enjoyed seeing our sons crawl back and forth over it singing, "We are Siamese if you please…" from the movie "101 Dalmatians."

We did need to instruct our children before going to the *Souk*. Shopkeepers would hand them something, thinking they would put up a fuss when it was taken from them to be put back on the shelf. The shopkeeper's method of selling more merchandise. Once again, I recognized how easy our children were to raise. They understood situations and how to behave when we explained. At times I may have gone overboard with explanations. One time in his teen years, our older son said to me, "Mom, you don't have to explain EVERYTHING!"

The rug situation was a very positive interaction. Sometimes the two cultures did not mix well. Sandra Mackey described that occurrence insightfully: "The Saudis and their Western workforce coexisted in a state of tension that was not the result of ill will on the part of the Saudis or their Western workforce but rather resulted from a combination of Saudi insecurities and Western insensitivities."

In my life, this took the form of men at times knocking on their car doors and yelling at me feeling like I was immoral since, although I dressed very conservatively, I did not wear a *hajib* (veil) and *abayaa* (black garb which covered everything from neck to feet).

Another illustration of the cultures not mixing well was the taxi driver who talked to me in a way that lacked respect. Then, as he was burning incense, I opened my window, and our older son said, "That isn't very good for my lungs."

Later our other son said, "That taxi driver has a very nice face." The driver spoke just enough English to know he was the topic of conversation. He asked what had been said. When I explained our son's compliment in my very limited Arabic, his whole demeanor changed. He was VERY pleased.

Two positive interactions occurred while we were looking at rugs brought from Iran and Pakistan to finance the pilgrims' trips to Mecca for *Hajj*. Our younger son got some big smiles from the Saudis as he toddled up and flipped over the corner of a rug mimicking the adults. They were checking to see the number of knots per square inch in the rugs laid out on the ground as that partially determined the quality of a rug. Later, when he saw a little girl, he asked, "Squeeze her?! Squeeze her?!" The people with her very much liked that and were calling it to the attention of all their friends. It delighted me when one of our sons made a bridge between our cultures.

Christian Fellowship

Both Muslims and Christians worshipped on Fridays in Saudi Arabia. The Muslims worshipped in mosques. We in a small underground church. Sometimes we met in the American Military compound, which was watched by the *Matawa* (religious police). Sometimes, when we were told by the Saudi government to be more low-key, we divided into smaller groups that met in homes. A missionary came in about once a month as a "social advisor," and our programs read "Sky-pilot Services" or "Fish-eater Services."

Desert picnic with Christian friends

Our Christian fellowship was a very close-knit group. There were not many children, so our two had many "Aunts" and "Uncles." They never lacked for attention but were listened to attentively whether the topic was spiritual or secular. On one occasion, a man asked our older son, "What do you want to be when you grow up?" Since I had just read our sons "The Elves and the Shoemaker," you can guess our young son's reply, "A shoemaker!"

One of the pastors benefited our family in an unexpected way. While eating with us one noon, he squeezed my hand three times after prayer. He then told us that was the way their family said, "I love you" to each other. That practice stood us in good stead when we used it during our older son's minor rebellion during his junior high years. The same pastor benefited me at the time by answering question after question. It excited me to learn about my new relationship with the Lord through the Bible!

Another pastor's sermon consisted of one verse from each book of the Bible. He was able to connect their themes so the whole sermon had a flow to it.

Most of the volunteers who preached when we did not have a visiting minister did well, although many times it was difficult to understand the words through the accents! Our congregation truly gave us the concept of the universal church body. White faces were definitely in the minority with people from India, Palestine, Greece, Egypt, the Philippines, and other nations. One Christmas, people from six language groups, quoted John 3:16: "For God so loved the world that He gave His only Son that whosoever believes in Him will not perish but have eternal life."

Some Fridays, we would all take food and have a potluck to extend our time together. Although we were aware of many nationalities, we were all very close. One of our American military friends would play praise songs such as "It Only Takes a Spark to Set a Fire Going" on his guitar. It was a great time of fellowship! My husband and I hosted those gatherings. One of our dear Egyptian friends remembers our home was always open. As she said, "We'd all say, 'Let's go to the Hendersons!'"

Although we had church on Fridays, we felt we should have something on Sundays as well, so we sang and prayed at our home on Sunday evenings. During those evenings, we learned Koreans were people of prayer. Everyone else, upon arrival, would begin chit-chatting, but the Koreans would sit down and pray before joining us. A like-minded American friend felt Christians should pray whenever they were together, so we prayed even after an evening of bridge.

Our children learned about praising God in that group. One evening our older son, looking at the sunset, cried out, "Look at that orange—praise the Lord!" "Look at that purple—thank You, Jesus!" I told a friend, "We thought he was turning charismatic on us!" It was just a joke because we fellowshipped as one even though we were of varying denominational backgrounds.

We had Friday/Sunday school as well. I taught in an unusual classroom, one in which I had to bend in half to enter as it was a racket ball court. The challenge was compounded in that another teacher had her class in one corner, and I had mine in the opposite.

Our younger son put a Saudi spin on the story of the men who lowered their friend through the roof to Jesus when the crowd was blocking every entrance (Mark 2:4). His interpretation: "Let him down through the swamp cooler," the air conditioning unit in our villa.

A very sad thing happened the week I got a substitute and attended the adult Friday/Sunday School class. I was very much looking forward to being there as I had heard the man who led was a very gifted teacher. Instead of teaching, though, it became a time of criticism on the part of his wife and a time of grieving on his part. They told a story of hosting a man who they had never met, a visitor to Riyadh. Somehow his accusation of the teacher was received by both and resulted in the man feeling he had been teaching with wrong motives. Whenever a class member tried to encourage him, his wife would interrupt, saying, "But you don't understand! He....!" and on and on. I knew at the time it was very wrong. I have wished since I had known the Bible verse which applied: "There is no condemnation to those who are in Christ Jesus." (Romans 8:1).

We also had a women's Bible study during the week. On one

occasion, I mentioned having read a quote from C. S. Lewis: "'I'm ready to accept Jesus as a great moral teacher, but I don't accept His claim to be God.' That is the one thing we must not say. A man who was merely a man and said the sort of things Jesus said would not be a great moral teacher … You must make your choice. Either this man was, and is, the Son of God: or else a madman or something worse. You can shut Him up for a fool … or you can fall at His feet and call Him Lord and God. But let us not come with any patronizing nonsense about His being a great human teacher. He has not left that open to us." Our leader asked, "What did He say?" Since I was a baby Christian, I could not remember anything He said about Himself. Now I would say: "I am the Way, the Truth, and the Life. No one comes unto the Father except through Me." (John 14:6) "I am the Door. By Me if anyone enters in, he will be saved." (John 10:8) "I am the Good Shepherd. The Good Shepherd lays down His life for His sheep." (John 10:11) "I am Alpha and Omega, the beginning and the end which is and which was and which is to come, the Almighty, says the Lord." (Revelation 1:8)

Jesus the Savior

Riyadh was a great place to receive Jesus as Savior. It did not come automatically to my husband and me. I had an argument with him during our trip to our new home in Saudi Arabia, during which he said he was a Christian because he was an American. I said, "No. You have to go to church to be a Christian!" In one of the early letters I wrote to my family, I said, "I will never believe Christ is the only way to fellowship with God."

But nothing is too hard for the Lord! One of the early witnesses given to me was a friend saying "Thank You, Lord," when her driver found a parking place right in front of the fabric area of the *Souk*, exactly where we wanted to shop. It was truly from

Him as, although there were hundreds of small stores, there was not even one parking lot.

I joined the Bible study her husband led as had been my habit. My husband had asked me earlier about a Bible study I attended while we still lived in the States. "Why do you call it a Bible study when you don't study the Bible?" We did study the Bible in our group in Saudi Arabia! When I joined, they were using Campus Crusade's Four Spiritual Laws material. There was a very clear presentation of receiving Christ as Savior. I knew enough about God to know when the Lord Jesus asked Him to "take this cup from Me" (Luke 2:42). He would have taken the cup if there had been any other way. So one morning, as I was doing my Bible study homework sitting on our bed with our two young children crawling all over me, I asked Him to be my Savior. He took me from a limited understanding to an intimate relationship with Himself, the living God. I became His child, a member of His family!

I could hardly wait to tell someone about my new faith and how it changed my attitude toward raising our older son. It causes me to smile now, remembering how I shared with a friend as we walked along the street in downtown Riyadh.

I did not realize until much later my favorite hymn before I knew Jesus personally was a prayer, a prayer God answered in saving me:

"Be Thou my vision, O Lord of my heart.
Naught be all else to me, save that Thou art—
Thou my best thought, by day or by night,
Waking or sleeping, Thy presence my light.
"Be Thou my Wisdom, and Thou my true Word;
I ever with Thee and Thou with me, Lord;
Thou my great Father, and I Thy true son,
Thou in me dwelling and I with Thee one."

Just as I came to know the Lord through the Bible study, I grew spiritually through it. We take having a Bible for granted, but a friend told me about her brother miraculously locating an Arab man in Riyadh who had been waiting for two years for the Bible which had been promised to him. When they saw him sometime later, he had given the Bible to someone who "needed it more than I do" and was waiting for the Lord to send him another.

My new relationship with the Lord was not apparent to everyone. Sometime later, I went forward at the end of a church service to indicate I wanted to turn my life completely over to Jesus. The man who had given the invitation asked if I was certain I had received Him as my Savior. But I could see Jesus had made a difference in my life. For instance, when our older son got bumped out of his place to enter school, it did not bother me nearly as much as when the same thing had happened the previous year. I was comforted by the realization Jesus had gone to the temple as a twelve-year-old, just as other boys His age. His parents had not hurried Him along; I did not need to hurry my son along.

After I received Christ as Savior, our Bible study began to pray my husband would come to know the Lord too. He had very little exposure to church and Christian living for his first 30 years of life. Nevertheless, he was attracted to the faith as he saw answers to prayer. God had answered, enabling him to put together a zipper he was trying to fix for me. He had seen our older son, who was afraid of other children, adjust well when he went to preschool. My Bible study leader, who my husband respected as "one who talked about the goodness of God and lived out his faith as he dealt patiently with high-level Saudi managers who were very difficult," and a Palestinian friend from Jordan came to our home one evening not realizing the Bible study had been canceled. After talking for some time, the Bible study leader got out the little New Testament he always carried in his pocket. He suggested he and my husband go to the next room to talk. The Palestinian friend and I prayed as my husband was led to the Lord. Our marriage was complete in Christ!

We do grow little by little, and one day, when I was grouchy and reprimanded our younger son about something, it made him so mad he gritted his teeth and said, through a clenched jaw, "Pray, Mama!"

Our older son was the third in our family who came to know the Lord while we lived in Riyadh. He had learned in Friday/Sunday School a song about Noah building the ark "but greater than all these things was when Jesus came into my heart!" He asked me what that meant. As a new believer, I did not have much I could tell him. I just said, "It means if you ask Him, He'll come in." Since the Lord wants very much to save us, that was all it took. The next day he sang a song he made up: "Hallelu for saving us from our sins. Jesus, Jesus, Jesus, thank you!" That gave me assurance he really did understand and Jesus had come into his life.

And he knew who he was! When he later asked what a baby's body looked like, I told him, "A lot like yours." In an indignant voice, he told me in no uncertain terms, "I'm not a baby! I'm a child of God!"

Although our younger son was not saved while we were in Riyadh, he was influenced spiritually through our time there. Since there was no nursery, he was with me in each church service from the time he was an infant. As he grew older, he somewhat listened to the sermon. One week he was so disruptive that I, with not the best mothering technique, spanked him when we got home. Later in the week, we learned he had been listening. He proclaimed while eating his egg, "People gots yokes." The sermon had been on the yoke of Christ.

When in preschool, he was part of a Friday/Sunday School class with children much older than he, where he learned words but not their meanings. That led to him talking to himself as he built with blocks: "Finished... All done... An idol!" Another time he placed something to represent a crown on top of a box and stated, "King of the Jews." Pretty funny in a shocking sort of way!

He also had a creative way of expressing himself at times. Once when he got out of the car, he said, "Spiders tickle me!" That was his way of indicating his legs had fallen asleep as they hung over the edge of the seat. Another time as we drove home after a Bible study, he and his brother lay with their heads at the opposite end of the back seat. His brother thought he was not getting his share of the seat and complained about it. Our younger son replied, "It's just my dumb body." What a way to express he knew he was mind and emotions, not just a body. Quite a deep understanding for a preschooler!

Spiritual Examples

The Lord provided wonderful people to aid our growth. A Lebanese doctor had come to treat the royal family. His private clinic in Beirut, Lebanon, had gone into bankruptcy due to others' financial mistakes. He worked in Saudi Arabia to repay the debt while his wife lived in Beirut, taking care of business there. He only slept four hours a night and once, after spending an hour giving our sons physical exams, he would not let us pay. "We're all in the Christian family," he insisted. He certainly acted like a grandfather to our sons as he came by taxi more than once during the night to be of help when our younger son had croup. Our children highly respected him. They sometimes pretended one of them was sick while the other held a stick as a make-believe stethoscope and "listened" to his brother's heart. During a Bible study, the doctor told us he had experienced the parable in John 14:7-11. He had taken the lowest place at the table and the host had him move up. He moved a seat at a time as the host instructed until he was the head of the table. He personified "count it all joy" in James 1:2 in the Bible for me. He lived joyfully even though he was used to having servants. He knew nothing about cooking, not even how to make coffee, when he arrived in Saudi Arabia. He said he lived in the grace of God. He fasted during the month of Ramadan when Muslims do not eat or drink anything from sunrise to sunset to identify with his Muslim friends.

An Egyptian we knew took the opposite approach. He left a bottle of water on his desk during the month of Ramadan to indicate he was a Christian.

Another Egyptian man and his wife were two of our closest friends. Soon after arriving in Saudi Arabia, they located our underground church. Not long after they arrived, while visiting a nominal Christian family, they noticed their children prostrating like Muslims in prayer. They were shocked and asked, "Why are you allowing your children to pray as Muslims?!" "We are here in a Muslim country. We cannot speak about religion, so we leave them for now, and when they grow up, they can decide," was the reply. That was all it took for our friends to begin the first Arabic-speaking Friday/Sunday School in Riyadh. Our friend was a doctor and had a urology practice. He only needed to work several hours a day. They spent the rest of their time serving the Lord, counseling, and visiting those who were members of their church and others. The people they met, plus parents of the children in Friday/Sunday School, formed the first Arabic-speaking Bible study in Riyadh. One day while getting dressed for work, our friend sneezed and immediately felt a very severe pain in his lower back. He was unable to move his left leg. When medications and pain killers did not touch the pain, an orthopedic surgeon suggested traction. Horrible situation, right?! But the Lord used what seemed bad for good. He fulfilled His promise: "And we know all things work together for good to them that love God, to them who are the called according to *His* purpose." (Romans 8:28). Our friend had been followed for some time by the secret police. One day they arrived to arrest him, but as they learned of his condition, they relented. He speaks of the way he and his wife were uplifted by the prayers of their brothers and sisters in the Lord and how the song "Because He lives, I can face tomorrow" ministered to them. When a Muslim friend told him he had been fired, our friend responded, "Thank God! We were praying for God's guidance, and now one of the doors is closed!" During the last Arabic meeting before they left the country, our dear friend preached from Romans 8:39, "Who will separate us from the love of God?"

Another friend, a Palestinian from Jordan who rode in a taxi an hour each way for church services, was watched by the secret police as well. He and his wife had to be much more careful about having Bibles in their home than we expatriates did. They boldly led a home Bible study for Arab Christians from different countries in the town where they lived. He and his wife very much liked Psalm 34:1 "His praise shall be continually in my mouth." He had been imprisoned in Syria just before moving to Saudi Arabia and fasted for several continuous days to object to being put into prison unjustly. Whenever I think of them, Luke 6:38 comes to mind: "Give, and it shall be given unto you…for with the same measure that you measure it shall be measured to you again." They were so giving that one evening, his wife made potato chips by lantern light to serve us the next day. She knew they were one of my favorites. Electricity was often out in their home. During those times, they would sit at night on the sand dunes where it was a little cooler. He was the one who helped me understand sin is so absolutely completely foreign to God that something really shattering had to occur to deal with it. It was not just God sacrificing His Son; it was God Himself choosing to go through that experience to break the power of sin forever. He gave everything so we could live the abundant life that comes as we allow Him to live His life through us. I was certain they would raise their children in the Lord. That proved to be true as they now have four grown children, three boys, and a girl, all of whom are committed Christians. I still have a vivid picture in my mind of him rocking their firstborn in the chair my Mom and Daddy had given us for our firstborn. As he rocked, he sang hymns to his baby son in English. When men like those three talked about praising God for everything, it was not a bit trite.

The Bible study leader, who led my husband to Christ, and his wife also became very good friends. She connected the Christians in Riyadh and those in Jeddah, another Saudi Arabian city. During a flight in a small plane, she and her husband were invited to tour the cockpit. The pilot pointed to one of the instruments and said, "That's what keeps us from going down." Her reply, "That's not what keeps ME from going down!" (to hell)

We also had connections with Christians who lived in the Arabian American Oil Company compound in Dhahran. At one point, we visited a couple who had invited Christians from Riyadh to stay with them a short time, generously providing us with some much-needed R and R. In general, we considered those living in Dhahran a little spoiled. After some had their doors painted one color, others wanted the color of those who had their doors painted earlier. We were concerned with basics such as how to get enough water pumped to our underground tank when it was not coming through the city pipes. Women were even able to drive on their compound!

I still, 45 years later, remember a tape I listened to by Reverend Donald Barnhouse while we were there. He commented he never had breakfast without first reading his Bible. "No Bible; no breakfast." I still read my Bible as I eat breakfast!

An Egyptian friend wrote a letter to a friend in his country saying, "You'll be surprised to know Christians are meeting in Saudi Arabia." The friend replied, "I'd be surprised if there was any place on earth God has not raised up a people for His Name." Truly Riyadh was a wonderful place to grow as a baby Christian!

Prayer

The Lord encouraged my spiritual growth by answering some very interesting prayers. One day I was in a rush to get to my appointment with a princess to give her an English lesson. Our son did not have any clean socks. I knew it would take more time to find them than it would take for them to dry in the heat. After asking the Lord to put both two toddler-sized socks on the top of the wash, that was exactly where I found them! The Lord had answered "yes!" We were ready to go when the princess' driver arrived.

As time went on and I learned more about prayer, I tried to "pray without ceasing." (I Thessalonians 5:17) When I was doing something that did not require my complete attention or when I needed extra help with a grouchy child, I would pray. I knew I could not do it on my own.

My husband and I found prayer was essential on a daily basis. One time on vacation, he arranged a wake-up call so we could get to the airport. He was concerned because the desk clerk had a lackadaisical attitude. The next morning when he went down to the desk, he saw a driver. My husband asked, "Are you going to the airport?" The reply: "How did you know?" He had come for someone who had not shown up! The desk clerk was in a panic, asking if we had paid our bill, not having heard about making a wake-up call.

Another time my husband used the subway system to tour the fountains of Barcelona, Spain. When he was ready to return, he realized the subways had stopped running at 10:00 pm, so he was stranded. Not only that, he was not certain of his location. The Lord's provision was in the form of a policeman who spoke a little English. He recognized the hotel card my husband showed him and called a taxi driver who united us again.

I also learned prayer is the guide to hearing God's wisdom. When I came home from being with friends, I found our older son had thrown all the clothes from his drawers around the room. I knew he felt I was not spending enough time with him. Realizing there was another place I wanted to go, I asked the Lord what to do. His solution: Take our sons with me. That was perfectly acceptable as there would be other children there. The only problem was our older son was afraid of other children. He went calmly into another room to play by himself but came out running when he thought he heard his brother yell for help. His love for his brother overcame his fear of other children. It was not long before he was playing happily with the others.

Our Bible study leader told us about reading a book that said, God always wants to answer "yes' when we ask in prayer. "Ask and you shall receive" (Matthew 7:7) in Greek reads, "keep asking and you shall receive." In asking over a period of time, ideally, we would mature spiritually. Our desires, therefore, would be more closely aligned with God's will. That made sense to me.

The Lord said "yes" as we prayed, then received a call saying there was a place for our older son at the International School even though he was third on the waiting list. The teacher told me later they had decided to take him even though another child had not left to make him a place. Since he had done so well at his nursery school and his teacher spoke about his intelligence and his caring about the other children, they thought he would be a helpful addition to the class.

His caring showed a humorous side involving a huge pile of dirt not far from our villa. It was a great place for him and his brother to play. He told me it would be a good place to go for Mother's Day. I responded it seemed more like Children's Day to me. He volunteered to stay home with a babysitter, "and you can go out to the hill and do anything you want." When we drove by the dirt pile later, he suggested my husband could drop me off and then babysit for them. It warmed my heart to hear him want me to have a fun day even if his idea was different than mine!

Our children also began a prayer relationship with the Lord. One day when there was a tremendous amount of dust in the air, our older son prayed, "God, please make the sand stop blowing so we can have a good trip to the sand dunes." A few minutes later, he went to the door and declared the sand had slowed down. He joyfully exclaimed, "Thank You, God!" His brother voiced his first prayer at the prayer group we had in our home, "Thank you for my Matchboxes" (cars). At an older age, as well as asking in prayer, he would tell God things that had been happening to him. It was really sweet!

When our sons began to pray for a car for our Egyptian friends, I told them, "You need to find out if they want a car." Yes, they did. Forty-five years later, our friends still remembered that prayer and the Lord's answer!

Our sons also learned about prayer from friend's children, who sometimes thanked God for all their "blessings." After our children began thanking Him for His "blessings," too, I asked what a "blessing" was. The older replied, "They're huge animals that live in the ocean."

Children outside our family also needed to learn to pray. And learn they did! We taught them in the Friday/Sunday School class. The first time a boy in the class volunteered to pray, he prostrated himself like the Muslims. Very sad he had never seen anyone else pray! After a few weeks in our class, he began to pray as Christians do. Is it not wonderful we have a Father with whom we can talk?! He so desires to listen and answer. "Fear not, little flock, for it is your Father's good pleasure to give you the kingdom." (Luke 12:32) At one time, we prayed for the Friday/Sunday School to double in a month from the three attending. Three weeks later, there were 25 children!

One of my life-long regrets is telling a youngster who was Druze (an off branch of Islam) he could not come to our Friday/Sunday School. I knew we could get into great trouble if it became known by the authorities. He was later killed crossing a street. My only consolation is in knowing the Lord cared much more about Him than I did and would somehow make it right.

We had a library made up of a list of all the books owned by each of us. We shared our books as we met for a Bible study during the week. One evening we were studying I John 1:7 "If we walk in the light as He Himself is in the light, we have fellowship with one another and the blood of Jesus His Son cleanses us from all sin." I asked how to give Him minute-by-minute control of my life. The discussion continued with someone asking whether God really cared whether you had fried or boiled eggs for breakfast. Someone else said he solved this by committing the day to God the first thing in the morning, trusting each of the tiny decisions would be under His leading.

I learned more about prayer in that group. I saw the Lord's answer to one prayer as He provided a babysitter both our sons liked.

I even led a woman to Christ who I had invited to our Bible study. I got a smile from her when I told her if she did not attend, I was going to ask her to bring the refreshments! One evening after a good discussion stressing there is a definite step of accepting Christ, the leader's wife suggested we pray for her peace of mind and then she prayed to receive Christ. We held hands afterward and prayed together. It was quite a moment!

Miracles

In addition to answered prayer, the Lord showed His mighty power through miracles to strengthen the faith of believers in Riyadh. One man told of a tire blowing out, which resulted in his car falling down a 6-foot embankment to the valley below. The car did not turn over but dropped horizontally as if it were carried by angels. He was unhurt and only the radiator of the car was damaged. Another time the same man's car was hit so hard it spun in a complete circle. His son, who was sitting on the side of the impact, was uninjured.

One of our friend's assignments in Riyadh was nearing completion. He and his wife were concerned about their transition to life in the States. Saudi Arabia had been quite a different environment for them and their two sons, aged nine years and three years. While discussing their move back to the States, her husband asked if she would like to take the boys to France to visit for a few weeks to rest and "regroup." He would pack up their household items and prepare for their return to the States. She happily agreed to the plan. It would give them several weeks in Nice, France, to become accustomed to the "hustle and bustle" of a city again. Sort of a reverse R and R. They rented an apartment right on the Mediterranean Sea and settled in to enjoy the beach and the culture and to practice their knowledge of the French language.

While there, she had an extraordinary, personal encounter with the Lord. They had to cross a six-lane highway to get to the beach each day, carrying all their beach "stuff" with them. One afternoon as they were leaving the beach, the Lord gave her an amazing gift. She looked both ways before crossing the highway. She saw her three-year-old son in the path of an on-coming truck! Even as the truck approached, she had a feeling of peace, of quiet and of calm. Then she saw Him! A magnificent angel standing between her son and the truck. The angel stopped the truck, a mighty miracle of God. Her son was not even frightened. She, with her other son, calmly walked out into the street where all the cars were stopped and gathered her protected son into her arms. Sidewalk observers asked how he was able to escape being hit. She was the only one who had seen the angel! It was a blessed event they will always cherish. I never get tired of hearing that story!

The Lord performed another miracle. He blinded the eyes of the custom agents as our dear Lebanese doctor friend carried his medical bag full of New Testaments instead of his usual equipment. The New Testaments were given to the Filipino nurses at the Military Hospital. Each was a wonderful gift as each went to a Christian nurse who had not been able to bring a Bible into the country.

In another situation, a man who worked with my husband found an available villa after a long search. The owner could not be contacted since he was generally in France. The housing officer had not been able to contact him. As they walked out of the office, the owner walked in! But there was another need. The rental agreement had to be in both English and Arabic, in parallel columns. Where would they find someone who could type in Arabic? Again the Lord provided. A translator walked in exactly when needed. The final hurdle was money needed for the down payment. The company treasurer could not be found and the company did not have the needed amount in cash. After deciding to try to get the money from the bank, really knowing the bank would not let them withdraw that much, they passed the treasurer driving the other way. Three miracles in one day!

The Lord granted me a personal miracle as well. Liquor is easily available in Lebanon but was not allowed in Saudi Arabia. Although I did not drink, I thought it would be an encouragement to our friends if I brought some to share as living in Saudi Arabia was very oppressive at times. I put a bottle the size of my fist into my carry-on bag. It was even licorice-flavored. One custom agent looked into the bag and saw nothing. He passed the bag down the line to the second agent, who also saw nothing! Again God had blinded their eyes! I was a baby Christian and did not know God's command to obey those in authority over us. "Let every person be subject to the governing authorities for there is no authority except from God." (Romans 13:1) In this case, the authority was the Saudi Arabian government. I should not have tried to take it into the country. I did pray "… let me not be ashamed." (Psalm 25:2) I knew there was a possibility shame might result. I did not realize if the liquor was found, it would be a situation much more serious than that. A week later, we learned about a British woman who had half an airplane drink in her purse as she went through customs. She was locked up in the horrible Saudi prison. I was very thankful as I recognized His loving care of me! He truly is Jehovah Sabaoth, God my Protector!

Sandra Mackey's Descriptions

Sandra Mackey, author of the book *Saudis: Inside the Desert Kingdom,* described the prisons: "Those prisons, unlike those in the States, weren't air-conditioned and had no TVs. A brief stay was usually spent in a huge cell with as many as five hundred people sharing one toilet. Those who were held for weeks or months awaiting trial were usually provided clean accommodations and adequate food but nothing else. Clothing, toiletries, and reading material had to be furnished by the prisoner's family or friends." She further wrote she knew her fate as an underground journalist would be a long prison term. And even if she were just deported, there would be the possibility of several months to a year in jail waiting for the Saudis to make a decision. To make her situation as safe as possible, she always used a nom de plume and sometimes hurriedly moved all her files, storing them with close friends and burying her rough drafts and carbon paper under the kitchen garbage until she took them to the desert to burn.

Mackey, as all others entering or exiting Saudi Arabia, was at the mercy of Saudi nationals who were the customs agents. No one of another nationality could hold that position. They did their jobs thoroughly as they searched for pork, alcohol, pornography, and products such as Coca-Cola, which were made in Israel. What they considered to be pornography covered a wide range of materials. Mackey further writes, "I had a book of knitting patterns mutilated, apparently because the models were too scantily clad." Who knows why one of the volumes of our encyclopedia set never made it through customs. The custom agents did leave the volume with overlays of human and frog anatomy, which proved to be one of our sons' favorite books! Interestingly enough, both majored in biology and chemistry in college. One became a college professor who teaches anatomy. It just shows what an encyclopedia set can do for a person!

The quickest our family ever cleared customs was one time when our younger son became sick to his stomach. I carried him right through U.S. customs saying, "He's going to throw up! He's going to throw up!" and got him to the nearest trash barrel. It was true but probably would have worked in Riyadh even if it were not true!

My Daddy's Home Going

The Lord showed me His caring love in what seemed to be a very little thing. When we invited people over for dinner, I did not have the chili sauce I usually made for shrimp. I found a recipe that sounded tasty. Unwisely I did not take into consideration it was a basting recipe and would produce a much runnier sauce. When I saw the need, I added a dab of corn starch, hoping it would not lump like flour. I saw immediately it was going to lump and prayed. I often prayed when I cooked. I asked God to thicken the sauce. I could feel it thickening as I stirred even though I was not heating it like one would a white sauce. It was the strangest feeling! I wonder if God was just giving me the assurance of His presence and control before a very hard experience that was to come. My husband came home with a letter about my father's funeral.

What a shock! The Lord took care of my husband in that a close friend was with him when he received the news at work. Then my husband was able to break it to me gently when he brought the letter home. The friend from work and his wife came over that afternoon. She cried with me. God in the Bible instructs us to "weep with those who weep." (Romans 12:15) Needless to say, I looked terrible in the passport photo we had to take at that time!

In telling our sons about my Daddy's home going, I reminded them how much he had loved them. I told our older son about the time he was very cranky and Daddy got a cold washcloth to wash his face. Our younger son remembered the socket game. My Daddy was not able to rough house with them because of his asthma, but he would shout, "Who's got my socket (a tool he used in his radio repair job and always kept in his pocket)?!" as they ran by his chair.

My Mom and sisters wrote about the many people who reached out in sympathy. That showed me how special he was to other people and the real gift he had for making even people he knew only slightly feel he was interested in them. It helped.

The letter from my sister, who was there at the time of Daddy's death detailing the signs of God's control also helped. She wrote he had wanted to continue the trip to see the new grand-baby even though he collapsed on route and Mom thought they should get him medical help. My sister was released from the hospital a day early, so she was able to see our Daddy one last time. God's perfect timing!

I did pretty well. I think it was finding there really is a joy Christ gives despite circumstances. There was also the realization Daddy did not have to deal with his body, his weakest part, any longer. I could imagine a bit of Daddy's joy on first being in Heaven.

One day, I hit bottom, feeling I just was not able to spend the time I wanted with the rest of my family. My husband was ready to take me home. I decided to wait a few months, as my Mom suggested. She felt she would need us more then.

Back in the States, my sister took us to the room where they had my Daddy's memorial service. I explained to our older son what had happened there. He noticed a pair of shoes and immediately said, as I knew he would, "And he left his shoes!" The Lord knows when we need a bit of humor!

King Faisal's Murder

King Faisal

King Faisal's murder about the same time had a great impact on the nation and on us expatriates. He was a wonderful man, very loved by his people and us as well. He was a man before his time in desiring Saudi women be educated. I was very impressed when I saw him at two weddings. He was a magnificent man and a great leader. He even began the 'General Organization of Social Insurance' designed "to make the State fully responsible for the support of the aged, the disabled, orphans and women who have no means of support."

One of King Faisal's desires had been to modernize the nation. A part of that was updating the broadcast media. When he became king, radio was little more than readings from the Koran. He authorized the building of radio transmitters strong enough to reach all parts of the kingdom and used them to foster greater domestic unity and a sense of nationalism.

Then it was on to television which he saw as a way of preserving Saudi values. All the local shows were about Saudi culture. Any imported films were carefully previewed and edited to ensure no religion other than Islam was mentioned and no alcoholic beverages or open displays of affection between men and women could be seen.

Sadly it was television that led to King Faisal's murder. His nephew Prince Faisal planned the revenge killing in retaliation for the death of his brother five years before. The brother was killed by Saudi security agents as he led a demonstration of religious zealots against the television station in Riyadh.

Wikipedia reported: "On March 25, 1975, at the Royal Palace in Riyadh, Saudi Arabia, King Faisal was holding a reception. Prince Faisal bin Musaid bin Abdulaziz Al Saud joined the Kuwaiti delegation that had lined up to meet King Faisal. The king recognized his nephew Prince Faisal and bent his head forward so his nephew could kiss the king's head as a sign of respect. Prince Faisal took out a revolver from his robe and shot King Faisal twice in the head. The third shot missed and he threw the gun away. King Faisal fell to the floor. A bodyguard hit Prince Faisal with a sheathed sword, but Saudi oil minister Ahmed Zaki Yamani repeatedly yelled not to kill the prince. Then bodyguards with swords and submachine guns subdued Prince Faisal and arrested him. King Faisal was rushed to Riyadh Hospital, where he was treated by an American doctor. King Faisal's death was announced shortly after twelve noon. A sobbing announcer read the official statement over Saudi radio: 'With great sorrow and sadness, on behalf of His Highness, the Crown Prince, the royal family and the nation announces the death of His Majesty King Faisal who died in Riyadh Hospital of wounds sustained in an attack on his life by mentally deranged Prince Faisal ibn Musaid Abdulaziz." King Faisal was buried in Al Oud cemetery in Riyadh, Saudi Arabia, in a simple unmarked grave alongside hundreds of other unidentified graves.

Prince Faisal was later declared sane by medical experts, tried by a court, and found guilty, with the penalty being death. At 4:30 pm on June 18, 1975, the sentence was carried out in front of a crowd of 10,000 in Deera Square in Riyadh. Wikipedia further reports: "Prince Faisal bin Musaid, wearing a white robe, was led by a soldier to the execution site and was reported to have walked unsteadily. Prince Faisal was blindfolded, and the large crowd watched silently until he was beheaded with one swing of a sword with a golden hilt. The crowd then broke into chants of 'Allahu akba' ('God is great!') and 'Thahar al-hag wa zahaq al-baaTal' ('Justice is done!') Afterward, Prince Faisal bin Musaid's head was displayed for a short time on a wooden stake before being removed by ambulance together with the body for burial."

What a grievous situation! Yet launching television in the English language was a huge accomplishment! For them, it was a source through which young Saudis could learn English and thus be better prepared for the workforce. It also gave the average Saudi an expanded view of the world. One example was an entrepreneur who opened a restaurant named "Apollo 14" after Neil

Armstrong's walk on the moon. A far-reaching change was forcing Saudi Arabia to adapt to Greenwich Mean Time, replacing the Saudi system tied to the rising and setting of the sun.

For our family, English TV meant our sons could watch Regi and his elephant in a semi-Lassie or Flipper type program as well as Space Ace, Penelope Pitstop, and the Anthill Mob. We bought a TV after one of our sons said, "I wish we were rich like the Abu Sauds and could have a TV!" We were not rich, but we could afford a TV!

Our sons and I were preparing to go to the grocery store when my husband came home with the news. We decided to go shopping as we did not know how long the stores would be open. Two supermarkets were already shut in mourning. We were able to get groceries at the third. I feared the possibility of a warlike we had experienced in Cyprus, but the situation proved to be in no way similar. The streets were very quiet. We saw only one military man. People later said the *Souk* area was full of military.

Our bridge group was given tickets to pay respect to the king's wife at the palace. We were known there as we regularly collected money to send to an orphanage. We sat for a little while when we arrived, as was the custom. The Minister of Protocol had just been there. The King had died in his arms. The man was either still in shock or permanently disturbed. He would periodically go in to see the queen and upset everyone.

The queen and a group of women were sitting on the floor. We each stopped to take her hand and to tell her how sorry we were. The queen's sister was there. I recognized a daughter of the king. While we were waiting, some Bedouin women came in from the desert to express grief for the loss of their "father." He was no remote figure to them.

King Faisal and the Bedouins

Bedouins personify the values of courage, bravery, hospitality, and honor. One of King Faisal's dreams was of a farming area where 10,000 Bedouins could settle and have a life better than wandering in the desert. There they lived in hot wool tents woven by the women. In times of famine, they sometimes lived six months just on camel milk. The dream was to be a city named Haradh. I found it the most exciting thing happening in Saudi Arabia. My husband's boss said he expected the clothing customs to break down there. They did not even have a mosque for the calls for prayer. But we celebrated Easter while we were there! There was not another Christian in sight, so we celebrated by telling our older son some about Easter and reading the story in William Barclay's Gospel of Luke. I feel honored in knowing we were probably the first to celebrate our Lord there.

A German company was hired to build the homes and irrigation canals out in the middle of the nowhere that was to be Haradh. There was not even a road, although there was a railroad that made it possible to take supplies. The homes were small but livable. It was funny to watch a workman putting up curtains by placing the ladder at one end then, instead of moving the ladder to the other end, just leaning over to hammer. Of course, the curtains were not straight!

Well at Harradh Agriculture Project

Our sons and I went with my husband twice, once by train and the second by flight in a DC3. I learned another Arabic phrase on the second trip. "*Tal. Habebe.*" ("Come on. I love you."), spoken by a man to his wife as they deplaned.

I had the opportunity to "talk" through gestures with a young mother. She asked with considerable interest whether or not I nursed our baby as she did hers. She was very pleased when I communicated that I did. Talking, whether it was conversation, prose, or poetry, was very important to the Arab people. Back home in Riyadh, it was not unusual to see our houseboy yelling to builders across the way. It seemed there was no barrier to cross like we have with talking to people we have never met.

It would not be easy for the Bedouins to give up their desert wandering and their camels. They were so proud of their camels they even had a beauty contest! National Geographic Oct 2003 states the right look was "big eyes, a droopy lower lip, a long thin neck, and a high fleshy hump." But camels were more than beauty for the Bedouins. They were transport and commerce while providing milk, dung for fuel and urine for hair tonic, and, when they died, food. They were uniquely suited to the desert because they could go without water for five days in summer and twenty-five in winter.

A brief look into the life of the Bedouin is seen through Frank Viviano's article "Saudi Arabia on Edge" in the October 2003 issue of National Geographic page 18: "It was just past dawn as Zafer built a fire in the entrance to the tent to stave off the morning chill and make breakfast. Teenage boys hammered out a drum rhythm in brass mortars, grinding down coffee beans to be made into brain-charging Arabic coffee. 'My

Camel beauty contest

heart is at rest in the Sands,' he said. 'I know how to read the desert winds when I graze my animals. I know how to find my way through the dunes at night by keeping *al-Jedi* before me. That one, the goat star', he said, pointing into the northern sky."

King Faisal was very generous not just to the Bedouins but to all his subjects and had regular meeting times called *majlis*, where individuals could make requests. We heard he gave one man a diesel truck.

Sandra Mackey wrote: "Faisal is by far the most interesting of the post-Abdul Aziz kings. He was both the best educated and the most worldly-wise of the al-Saud monarchs. Yet, he embodied the [former] ideals of piety and devotion. He wisely understood the need to lead Saudi Arabia into the modern world while at the same time preserving the sanctity of its traditions. Adopting the classic position of an Islamic conservative, he shepherded his people back into the future."

Return to the States

When one of our sons asked, "Dad, what's baseball?" we decided it was time to move back to the States.

Due to a change in management, we had a much greater shipping allowance when we went to Saudi Arabia than when we returned to the States. Most of the allowance went for the books my husband wanted to be shipped. That meant part of getting ready to return home was giving away some of our belonging to underground missionaries who had just moved to Riyadh. Through that, we saw the Lord keep the promise He gives in Luke 6:38: "Give and it shall be given to you...For with the same measure you give to others, it shall be measured to you." We found that to be true when back in the States, we were able to replace items we needed almost invariably at sale prices. When I asked, the Lord even fixed our furnace and saved us a repair bill!

We sold some of our children's toys, promising we would shop for new toys in the States. I thought with the great abundance of toys in Toys R Us, our sons would have a great time picking out a multitude of things that appealed to them. Such was not the case. They had become satisfied with less and did not have big appetites, a useful trait no matter what your age. It was fun to see that in both cities, Riyadh then Houston, one of the toys was a little wind-up dog that scuttled along, yipping as he went. I still think of our time in Riyadh when I see dogs like that at the kiosk in the Mall.

As for me, I felt a sense of loss when it came time to return to the States permanently. I really had grown to love the place that had become our second home! Having most of our good friends move back to their homes in the States before we did made it more bearable. We also knew we would be seeing some of our best friends when we landed. We would stay with them for a few days and see Disney World together. So back it was to the States arriving to find our luggage had been lost in transit. We were still the proud possessors of one comb and one tooth-brush! There was an upside, though. With my husband's foot in a cast from an accident as he taught a Saudi to drive a Ditch Witch, it was a real convenience to have our luggage brought by the airline to our friends' home.

And we still had our memories. Like the horse at the experiment station putting his head next to our older son's head in what looked like affection. Like serving a glass of Tang each time a visitor arrived as it felt like all the liquid in your body was being sucked out when one went outside. Like our young sons thinking a visitor's name was Kitab as he kept saying that when he actually was saying the word for "book." Like sitting with the mother of one of our older son's preschool playmates, who plunged to his death after climbing over the barrier and falling off the balcony of the hotel in which they were saying. Like beginning to memorize Scripture soon after, I became a Christian as I was meeting with a few friends who did. Like walking on the walkway of the city's water tower on a sight-seeing tour high above Riyadh. Like a visiting missionary telling me, "I don't usually hold it like that," and looking down to see I was holding the map upside down! Like our son having

Older son with affectionate horse

a "second mother" in a friend who took care of him when I substituted for teachers who were ill. Like feeling soft towels for the first time in months and months on a tour of the new Intercontinental Hotel. Like raising my hand up or down to indicate whether the children should sing higher or lower as part of teaching music in the elementary school until a qualified music teacher arrived with her husband. Like planning the Christmas program when I was the music teacher. Like sending the son of my husband's boss to the office when I substituted in junior high. Like staying in such a small hotel in the mountains of Cyprus that if we were not going to eat a meal with them, we would let them know so food would not be prepared for us. Like our older son liking his baby sitter to be "a long-haired one." Like remembering, "It is better to trust in the Lord than to put confidence in men" when we had a problem in an airport. He cleared the way when I chose to trust Him rather than to try to work it out myself. (Psalm 118:8) Like my husband spending time with Nobel Prize winner Norman Bourland when he came to Saudi Arabia considering a plan to use excess gas from the oil wells to make fertilizer. Like our older son turning over the bench meant to hold luggage, having his brother get into it, then referring to my husband and me as "Mary" and "Joseph." That resulted in a puzzled look from the bell boy and amusement when I explained the situation. Like my husband and I meeting a couple in Riyadh who were raised within a few miles of where my husband grew up. Like our dear Palestinian friend saying, "In Heaven, there will be no language barrier!" Like the best friends, we have ever had.

We were back at our starting point, our reason for moving to Saudi Arabia. My husband had no job! And how could one find a job from that distance? We decided to visit my sister and her husband in New Mexico before living with my Mom in Colorado while he looked for a new one. So back he went to New York City to finish his Ford Foundation responsibility, delivering a paper on agriculture possibilities in Sudan and Iran as well as Saudi Arabia. While he was gone, he got a phone call from NASA wanting to know if he would be interested in a low-flying satellite program that would determine the potential yield of crops around the world. We later learned his major professor at the University of Arizona had seen the job opening in an agriculture journal and told them about my husband. NASA pursued him to Saudi Arabia. Then to Washington D.C., New York City, and Albuquerque, New Mexico, before finally being able to speak with him in Denver, Colorado. He was just what they needed—a farm boy with a Ph.D. who could interpret what they were seeing from a satellite! The phone call was so completely unexpected that when I called to let him know of their interest, he thought I was speaking of a group in Sudan with similar initials to which he had sent his resume.

Since our sons were 2 ½ and 3 months when we went to Riyadh, getting used to a different culture for them was returning to the States after five years. I told our older son's second-grade teacher, "He can read anything you put before him, but you'll have to explain all the basics to him as he hasn't been in a lunchroom once in his life!" Later a teacher counted incorrect a question on a true/false test: "People all over the world are pretty much alike." He marked it "False" as he had seen multiple wives riding in the back of a pickup!

A plus of having lived in a country where there were many different skin shades was our sons' color blindness. Most of the Saudi Arabian population was Arab. A segment was composed primarily of immigrants from Africa who were brought to Saudi Arabia as slaves before slavery was abolished in 1967. *Hajjis* from many nations who had come to Mecca on the pilgrimage and never returned to their home nation made up the rest. All provided a variety of skin tones. The result was our sons' color blindness.

For example, one day, when we were out for a drive, we saw some boys playing in a vacant lot. My husband asked, "Which is the Rogers' boy?"

Our older son replied, "He's the one in the red shirt. He's got black hair." It did not occur to him to describe the friend by the color of his skin.

The color blindness also led to a comical situation as movers were unpacking our belongings. Our children were calling the men "the black one" and "the white one." I quickly told them they could not talk like that here in the States. The funny part was they were identifying them according to the color of their shirts and the skin tone was the opposite of the shirt color!

Children adapt easily, and ours did. It was me who had difficulty. I felt like I no longer knew how to keep house and other tasks expected of an American homemaker. I spent some time sitting in a chair just crying and singing to the Lord. My adjustment to my own culture was definitely more difficult than my adjustment to the Saudi culture. When we arrived there, people understood what we were going through. They helped us learn how to function. When we returned, no one knew what we were experiencing. As a result, I have tried to cushion those who have returned home from living in another culture.

I am very thankful for the time we spent in Saudi Arabia. I learned many valuable lessons during our time there. By far, the most important lesson I needed to learn was to have Jesus as my Savior from sin.

There were many other lessons as well:

1. We have a very present and active God.
2. The Lord will show me what I am to do if I take time to listen.
3. Christians grow better in community.
4. Being with Christians of various nationalities and denominations gives one a realization of the universal church body.
5. Family bonding occurs when much time is spent together.
6. Life-long friendships form when the hustle and bustle of life does not get in the way of time spent together.
7. There are various ways to do many things, like marrying and raising children, successfully.
8. It is possible to live with contentment in a culture very different than one's own.
9. Our lives are broadened as we spend time with people whose lives differ from ours.
10. It is fun to eat foods that are not traditional American cuisine.
11. Hospitality feels good. I enjoyed preparing food to share with others after church services, as well as being a hostess at dinner parties and having overnight visitors when pastors and others came to town.
12. It really is possible to feel relaxed in completely foreign circumstances, such as sitting on cushions around on the floor drinking Arabic coffee made on a hot plate propped on two rocks.
13. Communication can be achieved with very few words in common. When I wanted to buy gum, I pretended I was putting something into my mouth, chewing it, and then pointed to my stomach, saying *"Maffie henna"* ("nothing here."). The shopkeeper understood!

Afterword

Fast forward several decades. What does modern Saudi culture look like in contrast to what we knew 45 years ago? Torn between ancient traditions and the modern world, Saudis search for balance. I like Sandra Mackey's evaluation: "The most competent camel drivers in the world now pilot supersonic jets."

King Faisal's desire to educate women has become a reality. Government schools for girls opened in 1959. Within five years, more than 40,000 girls attended.

Education has enabled women to work in medicine, education, or women's banking and to be entrepreneurs but only with women. The dividing line between the sexes has not been broken in those areas.

The hospital which bears King Faisal's name is no longer on the edge of the desert. Instead, large walled-in villas stretch out from it in every direction and one enters from a 6-lane divided thoroughfare.

Haradh, one of his pet projects, now has a four-lane highway from the City of Hafuf and other highways going west and east. Instead of alfalfa, there now is one of the largest dairy farms in Middle East and North Africa, one of the major gas plants in Saudi Arabia, five restaurants, and even an ATM machine!

King Faisal's desire to give the Bedouins a more comfortable lifestyle succeeded! In 2003, according to National Geographic, October 2003 issue, about 600,000 Saudis still lived the Bedouin desert wanderer's life, an enormous change from an estimated two million a half-century before.

On the transportation front, although it still not safe, 97% of the beds in the hospital are no longer occupied by victims of traffic accidents. Signs in English such as "It is dangerous to think or talk while driving" can be seen. Humorous to expatriates. Maybe they helped. Maybe it was just in the translation! Drivers are more orderly, as are the airports where Saudia, the national airline, is successful in forcing passengers to board planes *walad y walad* (one by one), replacing the stampede which required we hold our sons to keep them from being trampled.

The colorful old *Souks* continued to crumble, being replaced by air-conditioned malls where many store owners prosper due to high salaries and the welfare state, which enables all to shop and buy. There are stores with familiar names such as Safeway and A&P. I found it interesting to hear an Arab Christian state he felt materialism would supersede Islam, after which the Saudis would turn to Christ.

Islam reminds unchanged but bold seekers can now use social media such as FaceBook, blogs, and search engines for organizations such as Global Media Outreach (www.globalmediaoutreach.com or www.witnesstoall.com/map and others. TV programs, traveling abroad, social media, and exposure to Christians outside and inside the country have also been a means of introducing many to Christ. Numerous eager Saudis have taken what they have learned as Muslims and, after comparing it side by side with Christianity, felt disappointed in Islam. The International Church of Riyadh states its purpose on Facebook: "Riyadh Saudi Arabia International Christian Church is a group of sold-out disciples devoted to Jesus Christ with the purpose of seeking and saving the lost." What a change from our small underground church! Our Egyptian friends from those days report when they tell their friends living there now what it was like during our time there, "They think we are crazy!"

The Islamist's (radical branch of Islam) plan, according to Samir Khalil Samil, Jesuit professor of Oriental studies at the University of Saint Joseph in Beirut, Lebanon, is alarming!

It includes:

1. reforming Muslim countries so that they reject the West and submit to Sharia law,
2. forcing the subjugation of Christians and other religious minorities in Muslim countries
3. and converting Europe to Islam from within.

They have the same plan for the United States of America. Wikipedia states that "the Council on American-Islamic Relations (CAIR) founder Omar Ahmad has discussed forming a lobbying group that would 'bolster our position in America with the U.S. Administration and other media and political organizations. This can be achieved by infiltrating the American media outlets, universities, and research centers ... if Muslims engage in political activism in America and are involved with Congress and public relations, we will have an entry point to use them to pressure Congress and the decision-makers in America." We need to be very diligent as wherever Islamists have taken dominance, life for the followers of Christ grows increasingly miserable and dangerous.

Not nearly as serious but alarming to their parents, modern Saudi Arabia also means "young women driven by chauffeurs tossing their smartphone numbers into cars of young men with baseball caps worn rakishly backward, their *thobs* tossed aside in favor of bay, low-slung pants ," according to Sandra Mackey.

Mackey also writes, "In every corner of the kingdom, generators for electricity are in place. Water is being delivered to homes and industries. Municipal buildings and hospitals stand ready to receive Saudi citizens. The rural areas have roads. The cities have cloverleaf highways, skyscrapers, and high-rise housing. Yet humor remains for the expatriates who live there. "The Saudi Arabian Public Transport Company buys sleek buses then puts one route number on the front, another on the side, and a third in the rear!"

Women now are excited about their newly given drivers' privileges. They drive on miles of freeways and boulevards in contrast to the trails through vacant lots we knew as we rode with our husbands. Just before driving rights were granted,

Loujain al-Hathloul, a women's rights activist, was sentenced to five years, eight months in prison for advocating driving rights for women, among other issues. Amnesty International reported she and other women suffered abuses in prison, including electrical shocks, whippings, and sexual assault.

There are high-rise buildings where men and women work side by side. There are streets with names. There are more than six million guest workers from Third World manual laborers to Western physicians and engineers. There is a generation with no sense of what work entails, raised in a system operated as a welfare state turning to extremists in an effort to find an identity. There are many young men with bachelor's degrees in Islamic philosophy who cannot find jobs. But there is upward mobility in which some men holding responsible positions in the government are descendants of slaves.

Beheadings are still practiced for leaving Islam to practice Christianity. If a convert is not killed, he or she still must deal with the death of family relationships. A speaker I once heard related how, even though he knew salvation from sin comes only through Christ and even though he knew he wanted to become a believer, he asked to have several days to mourn as he knew he would lose his family. He told us, "My Mother has never been the same." Then, as another believer stated, "Church became my family." Believers in these circumstances often become stronger in the faith than those of us in the West who have given so little to follow Jesus.

More and more Saudis have moved into jobs formerly held by expatriates and some companies have pulled their people out of the kingdom. Sandra Mackey wrote, "The Westerners have done what they could best do for the Saudis. They built a physical infrastructure and frame the organizational models for a modern country." It was time for the Saudis to take control. They do that, as she further states, with two profound questions looming over them:

1. How to equably divide the finite economic resources among people whose expectations were fueled by ten years of unbelievable wealth

2. How to turn a society turned upside-down by wealth and the invasion of foreigners and govern it as it struggles to define itself

Traditionalists believe much harm has been done to the nation through the people's contact with the West. They cite the weakening of the Saudi's religious values evidenced by fewer praying in the mosques and apathy and alienation rather than the former fierce defense of the standards of Islam. They are also disturbed by Western words such as "sandwich," "bus," and "radio" creeping into Arabic in what they feel is the corruption of the purity of the language of the Koran.

"What happens here in the next five to fifteen years will be crucial," said Prince Faisal bin Abdullah who is a member of the National Guard. His ambition is to establish a network of think tanks for Saudi Arabia, modeled on those he encountered professionally as a student at Stanford University. He believes only technology can thread a rational course between the dangers of both religious fanaticism and mindless mass consumption. Many in the rising generation of leaders share this conclusion. There is already a firm base. In the consultative assembly made up of 120 individuals, there are 77 with doctorates or medical degrees, and 87 are graduates of major Western universities. (National Geographic Oct 20, 2003)

What would the Saudis like the world to see about their nation re National Geographic? Oct 2003 page 40? "Not the hijackers of September 11, who branded the kingdom with the stigma of terrorism, but a heavenly ordered state in which mercy is a paramount virtue. Not the grim spectacle of a public beheading, but the intense faith that it can halt it, based directly on the Prophet Mohammed's account of God's word as revealed to him on the Arabian Peninsula nearly 1,400 years ago and recorded in the Koran."

We've recently begun connecting over Zoom with Riyadh friends. We saw in real-time our Palestinian friend living in Jordan who prayed with me as an American led my husband to the Lord and Egyptian friends who now live in Canada. There were fifteen of us on that visit. It was so good to see those whose relationships we still treasure. Technology is amazing! Many Arabs who we did not know joined us in the latest Zoom meeting. Those who left Riyadh just recently reported Arabs now meet freely there as well as get church services online. The freedom is somewhat limited as they cannot preach to the Saudis, but they "live what we preach and that leads to questions and witness." There are about five Arabic-speaking services with about fifteen people in each. They meet two or three times a week. All that must be done very carefully as it is still a crime punishable by death for a Saudi to become a believer in Christ.

Alhumdeallah

Alhumdeallah (praise be to God) that we decided to make the giant step needed to change cultures. You never really know whether a new place seems like home until you leave for a bit. It was good to find Saudi Arabia was our home as we returned from the States after our first trip to visit family. It was good to again see the familiar sights of men in *thobs* and even goats everywhere! Today Riyadh still has some of a home feeling for me. Rather than the old song "I Left My Heart in San Francisco," I would say, "I Left (Part of) My Heart in Riyadh, Saudi Arabia."

I have actually had two homes, Colorado and Saudi Arabia. Yet to come is the eternal home which is far better than either of the others. Saudi Arabia had its problems. The States has its problems. But the Lord Jesus is preparing a perfect, eternal place for me in Heaven, a place with no problems. His promise is, "In my Father's house are many rooms...I go to prepare a place for you." (John 14:6) I will live there forever in His joy. In the meantime, it gives me earthly joy to reach out to the many internationals who live around me in Houston, Texas, knowing they can experience peace on earth only the Lord Jesus can bring and eternal joy in the heavenly home if they will join me in living for Him.